ME AND MY BLEEDING MOUTH

The Painful True Story of Gary McCormick

SUE WELLER

DAY THREE EDITIONS
an imprint of Maritime Books

ME AND MY BLEEDING MOUTH

First published 2005

First edition

Published by Day Three Editions
an imprint of Maritime Books
Lodge Hill
Liskeard
PL14 4EL
UK

Printed in England by Bookmarque Ltd, Croydon

ISBN 1 904459 1 45

Sue Weller is a writer and artist living in Falmouth, Cornwall

To My Husband Sam

Contents

ACKNOWLEDGEMENTS

I would like to thank the following people who helped make the completion of this book possible.

Paul and Pam Adams provided the recording equipment and setting for the initial interviews I conducted with Gary, plus a delicious Cornish pasty lunch!

Mark Davy gave me an insight into Gary's personality.

Christine Tipper was an invaluable help in editing the manuscript.

Pat Smith lent me her house for the final days of writing so that I could revise and complete the book undisturbed.

Pat Garnett patiently typeset the manuscript.

Alan Street at Gardners Wholesale provided much appreciated marketing advice.

Publisher Mike Critchley coped with the progressive expansion of the deadline and many technical hitches in an admirable way.

And my daughter Zoe gave me endless moral support.

HOW THIS BOOK CAME ABOUT

It all started when, along with others, I was approached to suggest a likely candidate for a new TV series which you may well have seen by now (May 2005), transmitted by the BBC as 'The Monastery'. It obviously makes good TV to put the most unlikely person in the most unlikely situation - and let the cameras roll. Selected from many hundreds of applicants Gary was undoubtedly a natural in front of the cameras. But this book recounts the story behind the face on the TV screen.

We've published books on the Royal Navy for over twenty-five years, so this book has certainly been a very different project for us, but, when you have read it I'm sure you'll agree that this story just had to be committed to paper.

I have known Gary McCormick for many years and seen him on his good and bad days. He certainly has them both - but don't we all? Here is a man with a chequered past, a stable present and, I'm sure, an exciting future. I recommend his story to you.......

Mike Critchley
Publisher

Some of the people in this book have had their names changed for obvious reasons; others are simply anonymous.

AUTHOR'S INTRODUCTION

When I was asked if I would be interested in writing a book about an Irishman called Gary I had no idea what was in store.

I know Gary won't mind my saying that the first meeting we had was anything but easy. He was having one of his 'moments', when the demons inside him were overcoming any willingness to co-operate. My task, to record our conversations so that I could write this book in his voice, was challenging enough without an unwilling subject! But I knew he wasn't choosing to be awkward; bringing up the past disturbed him. You'll understand why as you read his story.

At times I wondered if I would ever uncover the whole of Gary's personality; he seemed to be a mixture of characters and I wasn't sure whom I'd meet whenever we sat down to talk. It was a fascinating journey! But fortunately Gary cares and I don't know how many times during our meetings he said: 'Sorry Sue, I'm not being much flippin' help, am I?'

We were a very unlikely author/subject match but we struggled on. Eventually I had enough material to write a book. Then I had to spend weeks living as Gary in my head; seeing his life from his perspective and digging deep into emotions he didn't even know he had.

I feel privileged to have been asked to write this book, and to have been trusted with exposing Gary's life for everyone to read.

Sue Weller

CHAPTER ONE

PUNISHMENT

'He's not bleeding on my new carpet. If you're going to shoot him, take him somewhere else.'

January 1986. The evening had started harmlessly enough in a council house in Larne, near Belfast, where every Sunday a crowd of us got together to play cards. Tonight there were fifteen packed into the fairly small living room, and there was a good atmosphere: we were smoking and laughing, telling jokes, playing around, winning money one minute and losing it the next. You know how it is when you're eighteen.

For once I was on a winning streak, and I was being cocky about it with the others when I heard a knock at the front door and for some reason I looked at the clock; unusual for me as I never did have much respect for time. But I remember so distinctly.... it was just before nine o'clock. Someone went to the front door and there was a silence where normally you'd expect to hear voices and suddenly all this fear welled up from my stomach into my chest.

The door flew back against the wall as four men burst in. They were in army gear, with baseball bats and guns; their eyes skimmed our faces from behind balaclavas. A girl squealed or gasped; you couldn't say it was a scream, and it wouldn't have been wise to scream anyway. None of us had seen anything like this before, but living through the Troubles in Northern Ireland you knew that if you were sensible you didn't draw attention to yourself.

They gave the impression that they meant business. *Heaven help the person they've come for*, I thought as a warm trickle ran through my pants and onto the sofa. I'd been out of nappies for quite a while but I'd wet myself because suddenly I knew who they'd come for.

Fifteen pairs of terrified eyes were fixed on the men. They stood in the doorway, looking at each of us in turn, and demanded: 'Is there a Barry or a Gary here?' Pity there wasn't a Barry in the room; I might have been tempted to point the finger at him, except that the guy who owned the house was already pointing his finger at me. He'd set it up.

They yanked me into the hallway, interrogating all the while: 'Who have you been mouthing off at? What did you say? Who did you tell?' The questions flew like darts, but they weren't interested in waiting for answers. Before I could say anything they started headbutting me as if I was a punchball in a gym.

My adrenalin was pumping like mad and it gave me the strength I needed. I had to stay standing: if they got me on the ground it could only get worse; if they got me on the ground I would be outside, in their car and probably taking my last journey on earth.

I thought about running. I was very fast on my feet and could probably have outrun them, but the front way was barred, while the back yard was home to one of the biggest, meanest looking Alsatians I'd ever seen, with teeth like a bloomin' werewolf. Beaten up or eaten up: what a choice. I stuck my ground and dived back into the living room where by now everyone was pressed against the walls or cowering on the floor.

One of the guys was right behind me and something hard smashed into the back of my head, splitting it open; I hit the carpet and lay there half conscious. He put the heel of his boot on my mouth, but that wasn't unusual. There's something about my mouth that attracts attention, and it's usually the wrong sort of attention; the inside's like a railway track, I've had it stitched up so many times.

I kept a bleary eye on the guy standing above me. His hand went to his side where he had a gun under his jacket, and he barked: 'If you don't come now I'll blow your head right off here.' I believed him. People don't joke about things like that in Northern Ireland. That's when the guy who owned the house made the wisecrack about the new carpet.

I'd stopped struggling; the fight had gone out of me. They pulled a balaclava over my face the wrong way round so I couldn't see. I can still smell it. It was stinking. Some smells stick in your memory forever: swimming pool chlorine; the disinfectant they use in school toilets; the reek of someone's filthy unwashed hair inside a wool balaclava.

Now I found myself heading where I didn't want to go, especially in the company of these guys: they bundled me outside like I was a bag of rubbish on bin day, except you would pay more respect to rubbish. A helpful shove and a kick and I was squashed in the footwell in the back of their car, with two pairs of booted feet on top of me, against my face and back and legs.

It's a thirty minute drive from Larne to Belfast and that gave me plenty of time to think. I thought about my family, about all the nonsense I'd put my mother and father through, what with being in trouble all the time. I thought about my brother and sister, and how much I'd got on their nerves. Then I thought: *Where are these guys taking me? Will they kill me quickly? Will they stick nails up my fingernails? Or drill my kneecaps?* All the time the car was jolting and swerving, and the stench from the balaclava filled my nostrils.

I'd heard of Heaven and Hell and I thought about that. I'd been dragged along to church for a while as a child but it held no interest for me. It was strict and boring and full of people who'd perfected the art of not smiling. Sunday School was much better; they had these parties where I ate as much food as I could and then threw up in the toilets. The Sunday School teacher smelled of chips and her husband looked like something out of the 1800's, always wearing the same suit with moth holes in it. I didn't want to go to Hell, so I murmured, 'God, if you're there please help me. Don't let them kill me.'

The car stopped; they dragged me out and pulled off the balaclava, which was now sticky with blood from my head. For a second I was able to stand but then they kicked my feet from under me; I hit the ground and the beating began. They started on my legs; the baseball bats crashed down on my shins and then on my arms as I leant forward to protect my legs. My arms went numb so I fell back and let my legs take the brunt of the battering. I waited for the crushing blows to my head, or the bullet which would end it all. I screamed and screamed, and they yelled, 'Shut up or we'll bash your head in!' I shut up.

For fifteen minutes they battered and pounded me, swinging the bats higher and higher to bring them down as hard as they could. It's a long time to be on the receiving end of baseball bats, a very long time. After a while you don't even feel the pain.

Then I heard one of the guys say, 'The next time you step out of line you'll get a hole in the head,' and it was over. By a miracle they were gone and I was still alive. I lay on the ground not daring to believe they had finished, certain that they would be back any minute. It was quiet, dark, cold. I crawled over rough ground in the dark and found myself in a field. Northern Ireland in January is freezing and my jeans and thin sweatshirt did little to keep out the cold. My arms and legs were beginning to bang with pain and I was covered in blood.

It was hard going, I had no strength in my arms or legs, so I crawled under some trees and lay there. The car came back, spun around and put its lights on main beam. Whether they were trying to find me to finish me off I don't know, but it left again and I crawled on my belly down the field, across a road, into a housing estate and battered on the first door I came to.

You can understand why the woman screamed so loudly as she opened her front door to find me, crumpled, at her feet. Her husband appeared behind her, took charge of the situation and helped me inside. It was beautiful in there, clean and tidy with lovely ornaments and nice furniture. I was a bit out of place, all blood-covered and dirty from crawling, but even so they lay me on their sofa and gave me a drink of water and a cigarette.

While they were phoning my mother and an ambulance, the guy next door, hearing the commotion, came in and said:

'You were very lucky, son. The last person taken up there got a hole in the head.'

≋   ≋   ≋

It takes a lot to impress doctors in a Belfast hospital, but the ones who treated me were amazed; they said I must have had bones like breeze blocks because my arms and legs weren't broken. I had holes down the fronts of both legs, and to this day there are great lumps of scar tissue where there should be smooth bone. The only broken bone was in my little finger where I'd tried to protect my legs.

During the weeks that followed in hospital I decided that things were going to have to change from now on. I'd led a really troubled life. I could talk for Ireland, and my inability to say the right things had led me into constant difficulties and now I had committed the ultimate crime; I'd upset the paramilitaries. They wouldn't let me rest after this; I would have to watch every word and every step, but there was no way I could trust myself to do that. It was hopeless. Why hadn't they killed me? What was the point of leaving me alive? I was no earthly good to anyone, particularly myself.

CHAPTER TWO

INTO FEAR

People try to make out that I was born into trouble. 1968, the year of my birth, was the year the Irish Troubles began, so I can see why you'd think my turbulent life was due to growing up against the background of the problems of Northern Ireland. I don't agree. To this day I can't put all the bother I've got into down to anything other than having a real talent for opening my mouth at the wrong time.

I was born in Larne, which you'll find tucked away on the east coast of Northern Ireland, north-east of Belfast; not far, as the seagull flies, from the coast of Scotland. They call Larne the doorway to Ireland; it sounds lovely, doesn't it, but with all the memories I have of it and the trouble I got into, I can't say I've much affection for the place; if I went back there today I'd keep on the move and go straight through the proverbial doorway with my head down and my mouth tightly closed.

Growing up in Larne, my world didn't extend much further than Sallagh Park, the housing estate I lived on, and our three bedroomed council house. There were three of us children in the family; my brother's ten months older than me, and my sister two years younger. My brother and sister behaved themselves most of the time but I was a right nuisance. It was always, 'Gary did this', or 'Gary said that', in our house.

My father was a hard-working builder and joiner; a quiet fella who kept pigeons. My mother was a nurse; she was the livelier, more out-going of my parents. We were working-class, not what you would call an educated family; I think the only books we had in the house were about pigeons. I don't remember seeing any others. My parents bought the local newspaper every week, to see who had been born, married or died, but I don't think we had a daily paper in our house. The rest of my family - aunts, uncles, grandparents - lived within reach, the furthest being my father's sister who had moved to Scotland, but even that wasn't far to go, with the ferry so close by.

We were a Protestant family. The word doesn't mean much to me; I'm only mentioning it because it's something everyone brings up in con-versation when they hear your Irish accent. Protestant or Catholic; as a child I couldn't see any difference. The family who lived next door to us were Catholic and they seemed the same as us. On our estate there were people with red hair, black hair or blue eyes and an old guy who walked with a limp. What does it matter if you're Catholic or Protestant, red-haired, blue-eyed or limping? It was all the same to me. Anyway, it's not as if you get a choice about whether you're a Protestant or a Catholic; you are whatever your parents are. You're set in jelly from the beginning, and I never heard of anyone wanting to change to the other side. It makes a difference to which school you end up in, so that determines who your friends are, but that's the same for everyone really; if you went to a different school you would have different friends, wherever you lived.

The first time I ever thought about these labels - Catholic and Protestant - was when I was about seven. I was always wanting atten-tion and had some very dramatic ways of getting it; on this occasion I'd faked appendicitis really effectively, doubling up in pain and moaning and the rest, in fact so effectively that I'd been admitted to hospital in Belfast. I was under observation, but obviously not so ill that I had to stay in bed the whole time. There was a wee park outside the children's ward and one afternoon I was sitting on the swings when a girl slightly older than me - maybe nine or ten - came and sat next to me. 'Hello', she said, 'I'm a Catholic'. I had no idea what she meant and didn't know how to reply so I just listened as she talked about Orange people. She told me that these Orange people were on 'the other side', so I thought maybe they lived across the road from her, or something like that. I hadn't a clue that Orange meant Protestant, but I sat there wondering what these people would look like because they sounded so colourful.

To outsiders it must seem strange that you can grow up in Northern Ireland and not think the Troubles have affected you, but I look back and remember everyone just getting on with life. You heard of people getting shot but unless it was someone you knew - and the only person I knew who was killed was a policeman from Larne - you let it go over your head. I suppose it was a way of surviving. Even if you're in the middle of a war you have to get on with life, and anyway for kids the most important thing is playing with friends.

The Sallagh Park estate was a safe enough place for children. We'd play out in the streets without any supervision, all running around together, the little ones like me tagging on behind the bigger boys. We did the usual things kids do, chasing each other, kicking a football, climbing fences to get into people's gardens when the ball went over. Even as very young children we became streetwise quite quickly. Sometimes I would go into the corner shop and see a bigger boy slip some sweets into his pocket without paying for them. Later we stayed at each other's houses and stole cigarette butts from our parents' ashtrays.

Although I mixed with the other kids and did the same things as them, I was an odd little boy. From a very early age I either missed opportunities or messed things up. It felt like life had it in for me from the word go. I was different from everyone else. My mother said that I had never wanted love or any affection, even as a baby; she said that I never cried and always pushed people away. She said that you wouldn't have thought I was there half the time.

I know that I was very observant; always watching, noticing things, because it did seem to me that the world was a very threatening place, and it was always the negative stuff I noticed. But I don't remember it being anything to do with the Troubles; I honestly think that was just me. I was a one-off. I had plenty of friends who weren't like that, however much killing was going on down the road in Belfast.

I just wasn't normal. This next bit is going to sound odd, but I'll tell it as it is, though I can't explain the half of it. I never *wanted* to be normal; I wanted something different from the kids around me. I felt I was in the wrong place, that there was a better place for me somewhere else, where I'd feel that I fitted in better. The earliest I can remember thinking that I might be able to get to this other place where I really belonged - was when I was four years old. I had gone to stay with my aunt and uncle who lived in Larne. My uncle was a long-distance lorry driver and I was sitting next to him in the cab of his lorry the day he was taking me back home. I watched him turn the big steering wheel, and I was thinking that if I leaned over and turned the wheel we would drive to Somewhere Else, to that other place, even though I had no idea what I would find when we got there.

I was happiest when I was kicking a ball around or swimming in the local pool. I was good at sport, but hopeless at competing. At my primary school I got to the swimming final, but at the pool they announced my race over the intercom and I missed hearing it, so I missed the race. I'd had a good chance of winning, and I was really upset because my mother was there to watch. I felt I had let everyone down. It was the same with football. I played in the semi final of the Cup at school, in goal, and then I fooled around and was dropped from the team. That was typical of me.

≋   ≋   ≋

I always lived in fear, too; always. Where does fear come in? I've tried to work it out a thousand times, because I reckoned that if I could find out where it started, I could get rid of it. From a young age it started in my mind and wouldn't let go; I was dominated by fear. I think I must have been a very sensitive child, which is a laugh when you look at what I went on to do - sensitive isn't a word I think either the people I robbed, hit or frightened, or the judges who sentenced me, would use. And I'm not using it as an excuse. I'm just saying that's how it felt.

Several things happened which could have caused the fear. My brother and I were left alone in a cot when I was about two years old, and he started biting and digging his teeth into me. Believe it or not, my brother wasn't an aggressive child, but I must have done something to set him off, and because I was in a cot I couldn't get away from him. It hurt a lot and I was covered in bites and very frightened and it seemed like ages before our mother came and separated us.

Or maybe it was when I was three years old. I was at my aunt's house and she had a wee hallway with a big front door. I managed to shut myself between the front door and the glass panelled door to the living room. I couldn't reach the handle to open the living room door, and panic came over me like an awful wave and I kept stretching up to the handle of the door trying to reach it, but I couldn't. I screamed and screamed and kicked out, and managed to break the glass in the door to the living room and clamber through.

Then there was the time when I was about four, and from behind our living room curtains I was watching two teenage girls arguing with their boyfriends in the road; well, that's what it looked like, but I wonder if maybe it was more serious than that because they looked really frightened; maybe they were being threatened. They ran away from the men, up the nearest path, which was ours, through the open front door and came charging into our house. I ran out into the hall, pushed past them and raced up the stairs where I stood at the top, screaming. I thought the men would come in after them, and get me too.

And so I tried to imagine what set off my fear, but really I felt that it had always been there; that I'd probably been born fearful. I was a square peg in a round hole, never fitting, never a part of anything, always unhappy without knowing why. The fear made me over-react. Once I went for a walk in a wood with my aunty and uncle and wandered off on my own and found the carcass of a dead sheep. It seemed huge. I was terrified. I ran back screaming and crying, but they were angry with me because I'd left them and they'd been looking for me.

23

They didn't seem to understand that I was really upset and wanted comforting. They told me off, so I was frightened <u>and</u> in the wrong. It was confusing.

Night time was the worst. I hated the dark and used to dread the light being turned out, but then I used to hate waking too, because more often than not I had wet the bed. If my grandmother was in our house she had a real problem with this, especially as it seemed to me that she preferred my brother in any case, and he didn't have the same problem. She'd get very angry with me. I tried not to do it but was hopeless; I might as well have told myself to turn into a frog in the night!

What a very odd child I must have seemed; a withdrawn, fretful, screaming bed-wetter. No wonder my family were fed up with me most of the time.

CHAPTER THREE

KEEPING BAD COMPANY

When I was young I looked up to the paramilitaries, especially the Ulster Defence Association (UDA), as my heroes: I loved to watch the Orange marches and imagine myself striding out there with the men and being part of it all. I wanted to join the UDA. I would fantasise about my gravestone: *Here lies Gary McCormick, who fought and died for the Cause, for God and Ulster.* I imagined being a UDA hero, killing IRA men.

I spent a lot of time day-dreaming about the part I would play in the UDA. It was a good way of enduring lessons. School was a nightmare and, as far as I could see, a complete waste of time.

For a start I found it difficult even to get myself there. My parents went to work early and once they considered we were old enough to get ourselves to school they would wake us before they left, then it was up to us to do the rest. I was useless at getting up; I'd turn over and go to sleep again, while my brother and sister would be up and dressed and off to school.

So I was always late and of course that got me into trouble. Once I'd managed to drag myself into class the teacher would create a spectacle of me, making me bend over so she could hit my backside with a rounders bat, to the delight of the thirty or so kids in the class. Then I'd skulk at the back of the classroom, either resting my head on the desk or leaning sideways off my chair, totally switched off. I showed no desire for an education, and it's a wonder I'd ever managed to learn to read and write.

Secretly I would love to have been top of the class, or even middle of it, come to that, but I didn't know where to begin to achieve that. When I think about it, even blending into the classroom without the constant teasing and being made an example of would have been nice! I can only remember making an effort on one occasion. The eleven plus exam was looming, and if I passed this I would go to the Grammar School, and that was something I really wanted to do. My granny, my dad's mother (not the one who didn't like me wetting the bed), lived near the Grammar School and if I passed the eleven plus I would go and live with her.

I can't remember when the idea of living with granny had begun in our house, but it had been something we'd talked about for a long time. Whichever one of us got to pass the eleven plus would go and live with her. I was closer to her than my brother and sister and enjoyed visiting her house; she didn't give me a hard time like most other people, so this was something to aim for. My brother hadn't passed so he was still living at home; maybe I'd be the one to get through!

Of course, it was a hopeless goal. I wasn't stupid, I came to realise that years later, but my concentration was so fragmented that I couldn't think straight for more than a couple of minutes, my mind so distanced from schoolwork that I couldn't retain a single useful thing in my memory. I also seem to have had a completely different system of logic from everyone else. My reasoning told me this: if you came first you won. It worked on the sports field so I reckoned it would work in the classroom. Not that I'd ever bothered to put it to the test before; I'd never been motivated to this extent. In the days leading up to the exam I spent a lot of time imagining what it would be like living with granny, getting all the attention.

If you look at it from my peculiar point of view, I did my very best in the Maths test. Maths had previously been incomprehensible to me but this time I knew I had it sussed. The papers were handed out; there were twenty questions and I raced through them. I finished ages before everyone else; as I handed my paper in I had a really good feeling inside me. I was bound to come first; all the others were still busy writing.

Out of twenty questions I got two right. By the end of the eleven plus I'd failed all the other subjects as well and watched the life I had planned with my granny melt away like a snowflake in the sea.

So instead of going to the Grammar School, at eleven I moved from Larne Primary to the Protestant High School, where we were streamed according to our ability; I was in the middle band. I was a bit worried because I expected to get bullied. You hear all these stories when you're young, that when you get to the big school you'll get bullied in the first year, so I suppose I was on the defensive. By now I was pretty loud-mouthed and fell into trouble right away. On our first day in class everyone had to give out their name and there was a boy called Angus; I'd never heard the name before and found it really funny and burst out laughing. I promptly got told off.

At this school I was open to all kinds of influence because I was easily impressed by older guys. And that's when my life started to go wrong. I began running about with new friends. I'd outgrown the ones on the estate; they got their thrills from fishing and camping down at the Skeg River, but none of that was enough for me. I wanted danger.

I began to get this strange idea - it filtered into my mind gradually without me even trying - that I wouldn't live to be older than twenty. *Nine years to go,* I thought. *Flippin' heck, if that's all I've got left I'm going to have to pack an awful lot into the next few years.*

I still felt different from everyone else; I was still unhappy with my circumstances. When I looked at everyone around me I felt special, set apart, but in a really negative way. To me, special didn't mean good; to my odd way of thinking special meant that I expected to get the blame for anything that was going wrong. How strange is that! And of course I did get the blame and then I began to enjoy it because being marked out as bad or having a reputation was attention of a sort, and I wasn't fussy where attention came from as long as it came my way.

The fear hadn't gone away; it was as if something was attacking my head from the inside. I felt as if people were after me, waiting to get me. I had 'victim' written right across my forehead. And as if all that wasn't enough I was convinced that I wasn't very good looking. Every week I seemed to grow a bit taller and my body was stretching into a long thin pencil shape. Adolescence was just around the corner and to say that I was a bit mixed up doesn't even begin to describe it!

⩓   ⩓   ⩓

So, this is me by the age of twelve; long, lean, confused, hungry for danger and, apparently, with only a few years to live. I knew I was soft inside and didn't like this feeling. I was determined to change and toughen up. Because I was sensitive I would need protection so I decided to get myself some by hanging around with the guys who ran around a nearby estate, called Ferris' Park. They were tough and streetwise; they didn't care about authority and they seemed to have a lot of fun. I knew I would feel safe with them. They'd be my armour, and maybe I could become tough like them. They were glamorous. If adventure and danger were what I wanted I only had to turn to them. Yep, that was it; Ferris' Park was where I would go.

It was inevitable, really, what followed. In running around with older guys I started on a slippery slope which took me disastrously downhill at such a rate of knots that I was never going to be able to stop until I hit rock bottom.

You can imagine what a laugh it was for a gang of fifteen-year-olds to have a scrawny twelve-year-old eager to please them. I was game for anything; I might have been full of fear on the inside, but I was reckless and daring and didn't care what they asked me to do. I was just desperate to belong.

It wasn't long before I had my first taste of real danger. We broke into the community centre, through a window, and stole crisps and sweets.

It was exciting breaking all the rules, and I felt as if I was part of a gang as we shared the spoils. We didn't get caught for that, but later that summer I had my first clash with the police.

I became particularly friendly with one of the fifteen-year-olds, and I'd stayed at his house a few times. He was someone I really looked up to. The only thing I didn't like about him was that his feet smelled. I don't remember him ever wearing a clean pair of socks; I think he just put the same ones on day after day. Even now I can still remember the stench of his feet.

He decided that the two of us would break into a tobacconist's shop near the estate. Because he didn't want to leave fingerprints behind, he took off his socks and put them over his hands, climbing through the window bare-footed. I followed behind, oblivious to the fact that I was leaving my fingerprints all over the place! The smell from the socks and from his bare feet was overpowering. My stomach churned, and it was all I could do to concentrate on clambering after him.

Then we were behind the counter, on our own in this dark shop, and it felt so good to be somewhere where I wasn't supposed to be. Here, I was a Somebody. I thought about the times I'd been in this shop, looking longingly at all the things on the shelves, with never anything much to spend, and now I was in charge, and I could have anything I liked. I walked up and down behind the counter as if I was on a stage, strutting and feeling so good about myself, helping myself to sweets and crisps. I found a knife and cut myself a big lump of cheese from the delicatessen counter. I was a king. King of the cheese counter.

While I was fooling around, the other guy was emptying the shelves of cigarettes. We stole fifty thousand that night, hauling them away through the window in a load of black bin liners.

I was given £15 for my part in the crime. When I learnt later that my mate had sold the cigarettes to someone in the UDA I felt brilliant. I was so proud that I had been involved in such an important task. And as for £15... it was a flippin' fortune to me at a time when my pocket money was 50p a week. The money slipped through my fingers like oil. I spent it on drinks, cigarettes and slot machines.

Now I was on a roll with this fella. I was useful to him and his mates because I was so gullible and appeared fearless; a perfect combination. They sent me on ahead whenever they did a break-in. One evening I found myself inside a house with a golf club in my hand, with instructions to hit anyone who appeared. My heart was thumping like a ship's engine, but thankfully the house was empty and the others followed as I went up the stairs towards a grandfather clock.

When we'd been planning this break-in we'd talked about where we thought people hid their money and decided that if we lived in a big house we would have a grandfather clock and hide our money inside. We'd seen it in films. To discover a house that had a grandfather clock at the top of the stairs brought the movies to life. I opened the door of the clock and groped around inside and found money bags, so it was true! But they were all empty and we came away disappointed.

We were game for making easy money wherever we could find it. I remember breaking into a car wash and filling the pockets of my parka coat with 50p pieces, wandering down the main street with great fat pockets weighed down with coins, swinging from side to side.

Obviously the police had been investigating this spate of crimes and they finally traced my mate. In Larne they didn't need sophisticated techniques to find petty criminals; there was usually somebody ready to tell who did what crime. My mate was already known to the police so it wasn't hard for them to trace him, but when a policeman came up to me in a park and arrested me, it came as a bit of a shock! Strictly speaking, at the age of twelve I was too young to be arrested and interviewed without my parents present but he broke all the rules, took me down to the police station and gave me a good grilling.

My first time in a police station... In the interview room I was scared but very impressed: the policeman relayed everything I'd done; how I'd broken into the shop through the window, what I'd stolen. I was astonished. I sat there thinking: *The police are amazing, how can they know all this?* It never occurred to me that my mate had told on me.

As the policeman talked on and on about what I'd done it began to dawn on me that maybe I was going to get punished, so I asked what would happen to me, and was told I'd probably get probation. I'd never heard the word before but it didn't sound too bad, not painful or anything like that, and thank goodness he hadn't mentioned prison. I wasn't too worried.

He let me out with a verbal clip around the ear: 'Get on home to your mother, McCormick, and stay out of trouble,' and I sauntered up the street really pleased that I wouldn't be going to prison, but suddenly there was my mother coming towards me with a face like thunder. She'd heard I'd been arrested - as I say, news travels fast in Larne - and was out looking for me. I thought she'd be pleased to hear I was only going to get this probation thing and not go to prison, I actually thought she might be relieved, but she went absolutely nuts in the main street, shouting and screaming.

I went before the juvenile court and got one year's probation. I didn't know what to expect but found that the process was enjoyable because it brought me lots of attention from a really pleasant lady probation officer who I had to see once a week at first, then once a fortnight. She talked to me about the things I did in my spare time and tried to help me plan other projects, which she called 'meaningful' and 'constructive'; these were meant to improve me and provide me with some worthwhile form of excitement. I can't for the life of me remember what the projects were - they certainly wouldn't have been my idea of excitement - but I knew it was in my interests to seem keen.

The one thing I gained from probation was something which stood me in good stead for years: I saw that my probation officer believed me when I seemed willing to change and realised how easy it was to pull the wool over someone's eyes.

CHAPTER FOUR

THE CLASS REJECT

I don't have kids, though one day I'd love to settle down and have a family; as long as my kids aren't too much like me! My parents couldn't do a thing with me. They had a go at trying to keep control: they'd come looking for me on the estate or in the town centre if they thought I was up to no good, but there was nothing they could do; I was always one step ahead. If they were on my trail I'd know within minutes; someone would see them, word would pass around and I'd sneak down an alley way or into a mate's house until they went away. If I'd been in their shoes I'd have given up, but it must be true what they say about blood being thicker than water.

By the time I hit thirteen I'd been beyond anyone's control for a long time. I had no respect for any sort of authority, neither my parents nor teachers nor the police, and I had no fear of any kind of punishment. I was untouchable.

I rebelled any way I could. I'd been smoking for ages and used to go down to the corner shop to get cigarettes for my mum - she paid for them on a tab - and took some of them for myself without her knowing. I didn't like the mild ones but because she smoked mild I had to. I got my first tattoos: there were no tattoo parlours in those days; I went into some guy's sitting room and had a swallow and my name tattooed on my upper right arm. My father noticed it a few weeks later and asked me what it was. I told him it was a transfer and he tried to rub it off. Later I had 'mother' and 'father' tattooed on my arms and a saint with a halo on the back of my hand, but it ended up looking like one of those lollipop ladies who stops the traffic for school children to cross the road. On my other hand I had a bird, but it was badly done and looked like a demented bat. I grew to hate these tattoos and now I've had most of them removed, and others put on top to cover the scarring.

Around this time I got the idea that I wanted a skinhead haircut. To give them credit my parents never stopped saying no to me when I asked for something, even though they must have known it was futile. The lads I hung around with had skinhead haircuts and wore big boots; it made them look like a gang, and I wanted to buy into this. I went through the motions of asking my parents. 'Dad, can I get a skinhead?' 'No, Gary don't you dare.' I went to a mate's house and he shaved my head and I became a baldy. That night I got back home very late as usual. I was supposed to be in by ten o'clock but to me that was just the beginning of the evening, when all the fun was starting. I'd ignore the curfew, spend half the night smoking and drinking with my mates and get back home at three or four in the morning when my parents were asleep. I didn't have my own front door key, and if I'd had one I'd have probably lost it anyway, so I had to get inside by other means.

Our house had a verandah running across the front; by standing with one foot in the letterbox I could haul myself up on to the verandah and get in through my sister's bedroom window. She usually slept through that, but if she did wake up she turned a blind eye. I did my Tarzan act up the front of the house as usual but this time, instead of ignoring me, my sister screamed blue murder. She'd seen a bald-headed burglar trying to break in through her window. That sent the house into chaos. It woke my parents; my father came running into her bedroom and went for the burglar in the dark, and started hitting me across the head. It hurt and I screamed, 'Stop dad. It's me, it's me!' He had a heck of a punch, for such a quiet fella.

I realise now that apart from wanting attention I was also on the look out for acceptance, particularly from my mates. It didn't matter what I had to do to feel accepted, the end result was worth any hardship to me or to anyone else who got in my way. I didn't understand that the best way to be accepted was to be nice; I didn't speak that language. I was into extremes; I had it in my head that the worse I became the more I would be accepted. My thinking was back to front. Sure, I got plenty of attention by being a petty criminal, but that didn't make me acceptable to anyone; well, anyone worth knowing, that is.

Around this time something happened which has left a bigger scar on me than almost anything I went through, and I include the worst incidents in prison when I say that. I was still being late for school a lot of the time, still being made an example of by the teacher, but now I liked it. Since I'd been mixing with the older boys I'd become a big mouth; it boosted my confidence to talk non-stop and make people laugh. I thought that by acting the fool and mouthing off during lessons it would make me popular with my classmates. My class was half boys and half girls, and there was an 'in' group of about six boys I would sit with; I always thought they liked me but looking back I think I must have got on their nerves, because I never knew when to shut up. I used to mess around in lessons and get put out of class a lot because I thought this was what everyone enjoyed. I had no idea of limits and always went too far.

One morning at the end of break I was standing in the hallway outside our classroom, about to go in; I was last as usual. I looked down and saw a note slide towards me from under the classroom door, and it had my name on it. I picked it up and read it. Written in pencil were the words, 'Gary McCormick is the class reject and nobody in the class is to speak to him.' I couldn't take it in. I felt sick. To be rejected by the kids I spent all my time with, every day...? I thought they liked me...? I stared at the piece of paper and wanted to die.

There were conditions to being the reject, said the note; if I behaved myself they would allow me back in the group. The trouble was that I didn't know what would turn them against me; it seemed that they could just pick and choose any bit of my behaviour and use it against me, just for their entertainment.

Imagine what it's like at the age of thirteen to walk into a crowded classroom and have no-one speak to you. I had to spend all day every day on my own; in classrooms, hallways, the playground, and all through the lunchbreak. Two afternoons a week we went to the technical college across the town for lessons, so I had to walk by myself and wait in the college on my own. It was so humiliating.

I couldn't tell anyone about this, not even at home; how can you, when you don't get on with your parents? They'd think I was exaggerating or lying. I couldn't even tell the granny I was close to - it was too embarrassing. I had a good mate in class but he went along with the crowd, and that was particularly hard to accept. But I suppose he didn't want any trouble, and at thirteen you're not going to stand out from the crowd and stick up for someone else, are you?

This had a huge impact on my life; if I was hard to handle prior to this, afterwards I became much worse because I stopped trusting everyone. The effects carried on for years, and even today I can find it hard to be in a group of people because I fear rejection. I'm not always sure who to be or how to act with others and I'm quick to think that people are talking about me, even when I tell myself that they can't be. Old habits die hard, they say. Well, mine certainly do.

The only way I could cope with being the class reject was to stay away from school. I would get my uniform on in the morning but then go to the cemetery and sit and smoke my mother's cigarettes. While I skived I didn't have to face the rejection but I couldn't do that forever; I got bored with my own company. Once or twice a week I went back to school and of course I'd get batted by the teacher, and the kids would all laugh and ignore me. It was a vicious circle.

Sitting in the cemetery on my own I tried to work out why it had happened. It made me look so weak in front of the girls, at an age when I was desperate to impress them. I felt lonely, worthless and useless. *Why am I so different? Why am I disliked so much?* I couldn't work it out. One of the boys in our group was a real weed in my eyes; he was a little guy with nothing much to say for himself and I couldn't understand why he was accepted when I wasn't. I remember looking in the mirror and thinking: *I'm better looking than him,* but then I thought: *Maybe I'm not, maybe I'm a monster.* In the end I decided the only way to save face was to become a complete rebel. Or, as I would have put it in those days, to become nuts.

CHAPTER FIVE

A VERY SPECIAL PLACE

I was in trouble most of the time; petty crime became a way of life. When I wasn't thieving I was getting into fights. I enjoyed quarrelling because if someone beat me I would have bruises or scars to show for it and it gave me satisfaction when people noticed the marks. At the start of the fourth year at High School my probation officer, who by now deserved a wardrobe full of halos for putting up with me, suggested that I should go for a short time to a special school in Belfast. 'Special'; I thought about that. Mmm... yes, I liked the idea of going to a special school, especially in Belfast, as I would have to travel every day. I liked the idea of travelling.

I was to attend daily for three months. I mulled it over, imagining what it would be like. Yes, the more I thought about it, the more I liked this idea. It made me feel different from the other kids. I wasn't interested in the reason I needed to attend a school like this, that in effect I was a troublemaker and no-one knew what to do with me; I was attracted to the idea of having an adventure and taking time away from the boredom and isolation of my life at the High School.

My probation officer told me that the school minibus would pick me up in Belfast city centre, but that it was up to me to get myself to Belfast. I rose to the challenge enthusiastically and to everyone's surprise started off really well. In fact, when I look back I can see that I made what for me were enormous strides forward at the beginning. I managed to get myself out of bed to catch a bus which left Larne at 7.30 a.m. Bearing in mind I didn't even know what 7.30 looked like it was nothing less than a flippin' miracle to see me that first morning, out of bed, dressed and on the Express bus to Belfast!

At Oxford Street, in the centre of the city, I waited for the school minibus to arrive. I liked the feeling of importance as I climbed aboard. Oh yes, did I like that! I was one of the 'elite' who had a minibus to themselves. We collected other kids at various pick-up points in the city: a lad from Divis flats and three sisters at Castle Street. I sat looking out of the window as we drove along, feeling so special. It got even better: when we arrived at school they gave us tea and toast, to make up for the early start. This was a bloomin' holiday!

I was a bit disappointed to find that there were lessons, but to my relief there was no expectation to achieve; the lessons weren't difficult and we were never pushed to study; the staff were more interested in building us up rather than educating us. The classes were tiny in any case; there were only a couple of handfuls of pupils, only two or three in a class, and at times we were given one-to-one attention. This was my idea of heaven!

My teacher was called Robert Clark; he really did give me the time of day, made me feel like I mattered. He lives in Belfast; he's a fantastic bloke and I'm still in contact with him more than twenty years later. I once said to him: 'Don't ever give up on me, will you Mr Clark?' and a long time after that he shared those words at his retirement do. Apparently, in his speech he said that my words had stuck with him more than anything any pupil had ever said, and that it had kept him going during the last years of working in a special school. I knew he would never let me down, but I knew I had to make an effort, too. When I was growing up he was the only person who had that effect on me. Later on, wherever I was, even in prison, he'd turn up to visit me at some time or other.

For the first time ever I really looked forward to school, and the days raced along. Some afternoons we went swimming, and on a Friday we would go to a farm to help out with the animals. I really enjoyed it, and had never felt so good about myself. It was structured and I responded well to that. On the way home one day I thought about what was happening: *It's called a special school because it makes me feel special, in a good way. I matter here. People notice me for the right reasons, not because I'm in trouble. At the High School I'm invisible and insignificant unless I'm getting into trouble. I want it to last for ever.* I noticed that for the first time I was behaving. *But,* I thought to myself, *it's not because I've decided to behave; there just doesn't seem any reason to make trouble.* It was the closest I'd got to working things out for a long time, if ever.

Ah well, at least it lasted a few precious weeks. Then the novelty of the journey to school started to wear off; it was time-consuming and I was getting bored with it, so I started messing around in the minibus. I picked a fight with one of the other kids and the supervisor on the bus told me to stop, but I ignored her. She gathered up my bag and tossed it out the window on to the road; the bus slowed down and I jumped off to retrieve it, and while I was picking it up the bus drove off without me. I was left in the bottom of the Shankill in Belfast, a place well known for violence, and I was scared!

I managed to find my own way to school by asking directions at the bus station. I arrived to be told that I was banned from the minibus. I felt a few moments regret and said I was sorry, and I think I meant it, but it didn't make any difference; they wouldn't let me back on that afternoon. Then I realised that getting myself from home to the school and back without any help would be exciting, so I turned it into an adventure and looked forward to another new challenge. From Oxford Street where I got off the Larne bus I walked to Maysfield and got on a train to Dunmurry and then walked to school from there. It was quite a journey and it took me ages. By the time I got to school every morning they'd finished tea and toast.

Christmas marked the end of my three months at the school. In spite of my misdemeanour on the bus I left with a good assessment. My probation officer was really pleased and I could tell that she thought a real change might have taken place in me. Even I dared to hope that. I'd managed to surprise myself by sticking at something and not skiving once.

In January I was back at Larne High School, but now that I knew what proper attention felt like I couldn't settle down. Nothing had changed while I'd been away; I was still the class outcast. The High School was rubbish. There was nothing there for me, nothing at all.

Skiving became a way of life. I would head down into town with a couple of mates who were regular skivers, and sit in a café or play the slot machines all day, or if it was warm weather we'd hang out in the cemetery, where we'd got to know the bloke who cut the grass. He said we could sit in his shed, and we spent our time hiding in there sniffing glue or smoking. Sometimes I stayed at home and watched telly because my parents were at work all day and didn't question whether I was at school or not. There were truant officers in Larne but they didn't bother with us much; we were beyond their grasp. We were too big to be forced to go to school, and they had pretty much given up on trying to make us.

I picked up where I'd left off, as a petty criminal, but I didn't seem to be much good at that any more. Two mates and I decided to break into a clothes factory, to get ourselves some trousers; I'd never got enough money to buy new clothes and one of the things I really admired was designer clothes. We didn't plan it properly or think it through; the alarm went off as we broke the lock to the main door. We assumed the police would be on our tail so in a panic the three of us charged across the factory and headed for a window. In the scramble to get out I caught my trousers on the latch and tore the backside out of them. I ended up in the road even worse off than before I'd broken in; without the seat in the trousers I was wearing, and with no replacements either!

Undaunted, later that week we tried breaking into a chip shop in Craigy Hill. This time we decided to avoid doors: we'd go through the roof and lower ourselves down near the till. There were bars over a rooflight, and although we kicked and pulled at them they wouldn't budge. I resorted to jumping on them to loosen them, went straight through the bars and the glass and virtually broke my backside by landing on the floor twelve feet below.

≋   ≋   ≋

Now that I was so well known to the police I had to keep out of their way wherever possible, especially when me and my mates were wandering around town looking for an opportunity to steal something. A glimpse of a policeman's uniform and I was gone in a flash.

One evening we passed a clothes shop that was known for letting you have things on tab; people posted the money they owed through the letterbox. There was an envelope on the floor of the shop's lobby, and by that I mean the space between the front door and the security grille they put in place every night to prevent people like me and my mates breaking in.

I found a stick in the road and we took turns in lying on the ground poking the stick through the grille, trying to slide the envelope towards us, while the others kept a lookout for the police. It was late in the evening; the pubs weren't out yet and the street was deserted except for an old tramp in a doorway fifty yards away. We couldn't reach the envelope; the more we poked at it the more it slid away, so we gave up. As we walked up the street looking for another opportunity, the tramp stood up, took out a radio, extended an arm in front of us and said, 'Papa Lima Four to Papa Lima Six, I've apprehended McCormick,' and the next thing we knew he'd produced his police warrant from under his disguise.

CHAPTER SIX

REAL TROUBLE

I still lived with the constant feeling that people were after me, and I don't mean the police; I wasn't scared of them. I couldn't put my finger on who these people were, they were invisible, nameless, but the idea haunted me and I watched my back the whole time. Occasionally our family had a holiday and any time I left Ireland I felt a real sense of relief because I knew that I wouldn't be followed.

The authorities were trying hard to sort me out; their next tactic was to send our whole family to a psychiatrist in Belfast. You can imagine how that went down with all of us! On the way we picked up my father from his work, and he didn't have time to change; he came in his work clothes, covered in paint and stuff, and that really embarrassed me. My brother and sister sulked the whole time because they'd been dragged along reluctantly. My parents were in despair and I had no intention of changing my behaviour whatever anyone threw at me, because to be honest I was quite enjoying the attention. So there we were in this psychiatrist's room with not the slightest chance of sorting the problem. It was a complete waste of time.

I had decided that if I was going to be best at anything I might as well be the best at getting into trouble, and managed that very nicely, thank you. It was one way of getting my parents' attention. The charges against me were mounting and I made regular appearances in court, the latest for criminal damage: I'd scratched my name with a 10p piece on a block of flats. It hadn't been difficult for the police to find the criminal; I wonder I wasn't daft enough to add my address and telephone number as well!

I turned fifteen in the March and in August the court had no choice but to sentence me to a month in Rathgael Boys Home. In England I think you would call it a remand home. It was an institution, similar to a boarding school; a modern block-built building about forty-five miles from Larne.

I felt like a total hero, going to Rathgael. It was an achievement and I felt important. Four of us from Larne were sentenced at the same time; I was in the junior side and the others were in the senior school. One of the mates I went with was a hard bloke and I felt safe knowing he was there because nothing could happen to me with him around; he would stand up for me.

In the reception area there was a strong smell of cooking; a nice smell, but later I discovered that the food smelled better than it tasted. We slept in dormitories, except for the worst behaved boys, who had single rooms; it was wise to avoid ending up in a single room because there was no-one to have fun with. At night they locked us in and we were only allowed out to use the toilet. There was a watchman down the stairs and wee bars on the outside of some of the windows to stop them from opening wide. In the mornings they got us up at about eight o'clock. The washrooms had six or seven sinks in a row and there were showers too. There were boxes, like lockers, where you kept your work clothes. After breakfast you had a rota and did things like washing dishes, or brushing the floor.

I found the experience exciting: I liked it, really liked it. The month flew by and I came out feeling like a movie star; the younger kids on our estate were really impressed to see me, they gathered around and I saw that I had gained some sort of status. Within a week the novelty wore off and the paranoia came back; I was on the lookout again for those people who were after me. I'd felt safe in Rathgael and determined to get back in there as quickly as I could.

I still had a load of charges against me and was waiting to go to court, but that was likely to take another couple of months. I couldn't wait that long. What could I do to make certain I'd be caught and sent back to Rathgael? Bearing in mind the problems going on all around us I decided a bomb hoax would definitely secure me another sentence. To make absolutely certain I did two hoaxes; one to the local factory and one to the town centre. And to make sure I'd be traced easily I dialled 999 from my mum and dad's phone and told the police where the bombs were planted. They descended on the town centre, cordoned everything off, and then arrived at my parents, house. In a moment of extreme wickedness I denied the whole thing and blamed it on my sister, even though the call had been made by a boy. My sister went into hysterics, and my parents didn't seem that pleased either.

I got what I wanted; a month later I was back in Rathgael. But this time I found it wasn't so good; I was sentenced to a one in three, meaning I would do at least one year in this place and possibly three. I hadn't expected such a long sentence and was not at all impressed; I couldn't see myself sticking at it for a half a year, let alone three.

I quickly got into trouble. As part of the routine at Rathgael we went to the chapel every morning. The last time I'd been to anything resembling a church was as a lad and I had no respect for it: I was expected to shut up and stay still, and that bored me rigid. And boredom always led to trouble. I looked around the chapel to see what was going on and where I could make a nuisance of myself. I focussed on the back of a guy in the next row of pews. I can't remember why I chose him; he probably had a haircut I didn't approve of, or something like that. It didn't matter; I wanted to pick a fight so I poked him in the back and called him a rude name. Within seconds we were fighting; I had him by the hair over the top of the pew, and suddenly I was aware of someone beside me. One of the teachers from the woodwork shop was stood at the end of the row, looking down, with his hands raised like an old-fashioned boxer. 'C'mon, McCormick, box me.' I didn't. I wasn't that daft; he was bigger than me.

After a few weeks no-one could control me; I was in endless fights, being unruly, causing trouble and not doing what I was told. I was angry and bored and restless. The officers isolated me in a single room with a caged window, and I was assigned to a psychologist who specialised in hypnotherapy. He was an insignificant, puny little fella with glasses. I wasn't going to let anyone get inside my mind so when he asked me a load of questions in a very quiet voice I pretended to be hypnotised. I couldn't keep it up for long, and burst out laughing. I loved the look of surprise on his face when he realised it hadn't worked.

I found myself arguing endlessly with anyone I came across. One morning I was taking my turn to do the breakfast dishes when I got into a scuffle with another lad. Suddenly two care workers came up behind me and manhandled me back to my room, shut the door and left me there. This was so unexpected it shook me up more than if they'd attacked me. I sat on my bed wondering what was happening, and before long the police came in, handcuffed me and took me out to their car.

The police! What was going on? I hadn't a clue where they were taking me, what was going to happen... and I was really worried because my mother was due to visit that afternoon and I didn't want her to have a wasted journey. In the police car I demanded, 'What are you doing? Where are you taking me?' I didn't like the reply: 'It's the young offenders centre for you, McCormick.'

This was serious stuff. For 'young offenders centre' read 'prison'. The place looked like a prison; it had a prison gate, bars on the windows, a high perimeter wall. I was terrified. I was fifteen, arriving at a prison. It was a big shock and in the car all I could think was, *Well done Gary, is this the kind of adventure you were really looking for?*

Everything happened so quickly. The car stopped inside the prison gates and they took me into the reception area and suddenly there was a prison officer's face looming up within inches of mine; he was screaming orders at me. I was petrified. He handed me a tube of cream and ordered me to strip off and take a shower. I had to smear the cream, which had a revolting smell, over me in case I had body lice. I

48

was given a pair of prison issue jeans, a brown and white striped shirt and a pair of plimsoll trainers, the nasty cheap sort you could get in a supermarket for 99p. From the shower I was taken to a wee cubicle.

They read out a number; my prison identification number. I was supposed to repeat it on demand but I couldn't remember it; I had no head for figures at the best of times and couldn't recall it however hard I tried. And believe me I did try, because whenever they felt like it the officers could throw open the door of my cubicle and scream at me and I was supposed to jump up and repeat this number. It would have helped a lot if I could remember it, but it did my head in; I couldn't make it stick in my mind. I tried and tried. *McCormick 5-4-8-1-1-0-7. McCormick 5-4-1-0-7-5-1.* It came out different every time.

I was sentenced to a five week order, a short, sharp, shock treatment designed to put the fear of God into you. The aim of the young offenders centre is to calm you down, to get you under some sort of control, but I was so angry inside that nothing would make a difference, absolutely nothing. From the reception area I was moved to the junior remand unit where everybody's under sixteen; you're not allowed to smoke and I could see it wasn't going to be easy to break the rules in this place. Those five weeks stretched ahead like five years. I couldn't imagine how I would ever stick it, but I decided that it would pay to behave.

Within the first week I was in front of the governor for mouthing obscenities at an officer. He couldn't take any remission off me because I was in there for such a short time, so he gave me three days 'on the boards', or in other words, in solitary confinement.

Three days, seventy-two long hours, in a bare cell with a high window I couldn't hope to reach, a bed made out of a big piece of wood nailed to the floor, and a pot to pee in. At night time they provided a blanket and mattress. The days were tough and endless but the nights were terrifying. I was still petrified of the dark and would cower under the blankets, afraid to look out in case I saw ghosts.

The only thing you can do in solitary is think. *Why can't you stay out of trouble, Gary?* I couldn't answer that one, hard as I tried. I knew it

49

was my problem; I never tried to blame anyone else for the way I was, but I couldn't work out the reasons. *Why, out of all your friends, are you the one who ends up going further than anyone else? Thinking of friends, I wonder what they're doing at the moment?* Lying on the hard board I pictured my mates in school or wandering around town or sitting in a café smoking.

It was good to have the company of my thoughts but I discovered that my thoughts had a life of their own: it was as if they got up on stage and spoke to me. They were very convincing, insisting that three days on the boards would be enough to stop me from getting into trouble again; that after this I really would turn over a new leaf. And, do you know, I believed them.

After seventy-two hours on my own it was wonderful to see people and talk to them again. It had been a salutary lesson and I was determined to tow the line until the five weeks were up. Some hope. During that short space of time I ended up in solitary on three occasions. By the end of that I was convinced I could never change. Crime was my life. There was no way out. This was all I would ever be, ever <u>could</u> be.

CHAPTER SEVEN

NIGHT OF MADNESS

From the young offenders centre I was sent back at Rathgael, to continue the previous sentence. They put me in the reception area so that they could assess me, and decide where to send me next. There was nothing to look forward to; I was bored and depressed. The days stretched endlessly ahead with no prospect of excitement. I started getting into fights again, so they sent me to House Four, which was also known as the rubber house. I was quite glad because it was different from the other houses and again that made me feel special. There were only four of us in this house and we weren't allowed out into the grounds; we had to exercise in a wee yard.

Sometimes it felt like home, sometimes it didn't. We used to listen to the radio Charts on a Sunday evening; we'd lie out in the hallway, and that was good, that was one of those rare moments when life felt normal. But the thing I hated about House Four was that the beds, which had a steel frame and a mattress, were drilled to the floor. You couldn't have anything personal to make it look like a proper bedroom. Obviously I hadn't told anyone else I was scared of the dark and at night when we were locked in, and the others were asleep, I would imagine all sorts of things prowling around the room. It used to take me ages to get to sleep. The lights were monitored from a central point by a night watchman and so when they went out at 10.30 they were off right through to the next morning.

During the day I had one-to-one tuition and the attention paid off: I behaved, and after a few weeks of good behaviour I'd earned myself a day trip back to Larne, accompanied by one of the officers. We were going to meet my parents to see whether it would be possible for me to go home for a weekend, but as the officer was also a referee assessor for the Irish League we went to a football match in Larne, and that was a real novelty. I made sure I behaved myself.

We met my parents at home and there was a discussion about what the rules and regulations would be if I were to return. I was told that if I wanted to come home for a weekend I would have to abide by the rules. I never did what I was told when I was at home, never, but last time I'd been living there I'd become a real nightmare, and if I didn't get my own way I thought nothing of smashing things in the house. But of course I agreed to abide by the rules. I was extremely well-behaved during my day out. My parents must have been relieved; maybe they thought I had turned over a new leaf. A date was set for my weekend break, and I'd like to think my parents were looking forward to it, though if I'd been them I would have felt very apprehensive.

Of course, once I got back home I broke all the rules right away. I had no intention of keeping them; they were designed to curtail my freedom, to stop my enjoyment. I had to be in at a certain time; I had to do this; I wasn't allowed to do that. No way - I had other plans. I'd decided I wasn't going back to Rathgael; I'd had enough of it.

I met up with a mate who had a flat. He said I could stay with him for a while so when I was supposed to be going down to the train to go back to the boys home I went to his flat instead and hid there. It was in a highrise building and the flat was dirty and very rundown but who was I to be fussy?

A policeman came looking for me, with my father in tow; they hammered on the door so my mate and I had to find somewhere for me to hide, pretty quickly. The flat had a really big airing cupboard, and as we had no money for electricity the tank was cold. I was skinny enough to climb in behind the tank, and leaned over the top of it with my arms around the sides. My mate threw a blanket over me and answered the door. They searched the flat, certain they would find me, though my mate kept saying: 'No, Mr McCormick, no, Constable, I haven't see Gary for ages.' They looked everywhere, even in the airing cupboard, but I was invisible. They left, puzzled.

I needed two things: a haircut and some money. My mate said he could do the haircut and I thought it would be good to have a Mohican so he cut most of my hair off, leaving a bit right down the middle of my head.

As far as money was concerned, while I'd been at home that weekend I'd stolen one of my mum's blank cheques, and made it out for £25. I did the best job I could of forging her signature, and went down to the bank with all the confidence in the world. The cashier took one look at me, my haircut, the hopeless forgery of my mum's signature and said very sweetly, 'Could you wait there a minute please?' and I knew there was no chance of cashing it. Before she could return with the manager I was out of the bank and heading back to my mate's flat.

We had to come up with another plan. My mate had a ferry and rail ticket to London so we decided that I would use it, and that he'd follow once he'd raised enough money to buy another ticket. London sounded glamorous and exciting; I could earn loads of money there. No-one would know me so maybe I could start a new life. I got together a bagful of clothes by borrowing some off his brother, shaved the rest of my hair off so I would look older and harder, scrounged a tenner off someone, and started off to the dock to catch the ferry.

But by the time I got to the harbour I'd had second thoughts. Planning the adventure had been fun, but while I was walking down the road I'd worked out that £10 wasn't going to take me very far. I turned around and went back to my mate's flat and it was stone cold, there was no food, and I suddenly saw how grim it was. Once again Rathgael seemed a much better prospect - at least it was warm - so I just went down to the police station and handed myself in.

A week later they sent me to the senior school for the first time, but I couldn't settle to anything. What was the point of schoolwork, which I'd never benefit from? I couldn't raise any interest in the lessons; most of the time I made excuses to miss them by pretending to be sick, and nobody forced me to go. I was more interested in using my hands; I asked if I could go into the painting and decorating workshop, and found I enjoyed learning these new skills. I had a good teacher who taught everything very thoroughly, and I loved it. It was a welcome distraction from schoolwork and made it easier for me to stay out of trouble, so I spent a lot of time in there.

I tried to keep a low profile, and managed to stay out of trouble most of the time. By July they decided I could be let out for summer leave and I asked if I could go on a youth training programme. Surprisingly they agreed, so I joined a project in Whitehead restoring trains, and was paid £25 a week for the pleasure. I had to give my parents half for keep, but still it was good to have some money in my pocket again; money for alcohol and cigarettes.

It lasted until I heard that Rangers were playing in the UFFA Cup in Dublin against the Bohemians. I asked my mum if it was OK if I went to the match. 'No, Gary, of course you can't,' she replied. 'You've got to go to work.' That morning my mum got me out of bed and I left home as usual but I went down and sat in the park until the off licence opened. I'd spent all my money so I stole a box of wine and got drunk and then scrounged enough money off a mate to get the bus down to the football ground and to buy a ticket for the match.

That night a riot started in the stadium between the police and Ranger supporters, and the crowd were pelting the police with money. Because I was skint I was running around picking up the money like the little kids do. Normally I wouldn't be able to resist getting stuck in with the rioters, but there I was filling my pockets to the brim with coins. We could only leave the ground by stooping beneath the tunnel of police shields that they beat with their batons, making a noise to wake the dead. It was thrilling.

I got back in the early hours of the morning, and when I arrived home my mother told me she'd had enough, I could see from her face that she meant it. Later that day she rang Rathgael and they gave me a last warning; any more trouble and I would be back inside. The words had no impact on me; I was living for each day and didn't care what happened to me. At the end of that week I spent my earnings on drink, went into a shop and stole a jumper because I was cold, was promptly arrested by the police for shoplifting, and soon I was back in the boys home.

This time I really wasn't happy to be back. I was the age now where my mates had left school so it was hard settling into the structure of the whole thing; I'd done it all before so it held no excitement or novelty for me. I wanted to be free; free to self-destruct. Also, while I'd been out I had met a girl I really liked and I didn't know whether she'd go on being my girlfriend while I was inside. She started writing to me and came up with my mother to visit me.

Time passed and I kept my mouth shut as much as I could and concentrated on working at painting and decorating; it distracted me from myself and my disastrous life. I felt a sense of purpose while I was in the workshop. Christmas was coming round and I was being allowed out at weekends again and then... I don't know what happened, I don't know why I did it; maybe I just couldn't stand the thought of Christmas and being away from the institution, facing my family and things inevitably going wrong: whatever the reason, I got in a fight and punched one of the other blokes and so I lost some of my Christmas leave. They took three days off me, and instead of going out on the Friday I had to stay inside until the Monday. I'd planned to go to a party on the Saturday with my new girlfriend. I pleaded with them to let me go but they wouldn't and I felt really low, even though I'd caused it and deserved to be punished. I couldn't understand how I'd managed to sabotage my chances again.

My parents were moving house at this time and when I got home they were at a new address. They'd worked hard and saved enough money for a deposit on a house, so they moved from Sallagh Park to a private road called Greenland Crescent. They were very proud of their new home, as it was the first one they had owned. I tried to respect it because I knew it meant so much to them, and the Christmas period passed without any mishaps.

≈ ≈ ≈

I was out of the rubber house now, back in an ordinary dorm with five other lads, and we were pretty bored and restless. In January the house staff took a group of us out to a shopping centre and we stole glue so that we could have a sniffing session once we were locked in for the night. Sniffing the glue made us feel invincible, and someone suggested that we should break out. We all thought that was a brilliant thing to do; we hadn't anything to lose. We flung the dorm rubbish bin through the window - you'd think the breaking of glass would have brought someone running to see what was happening but we were out on the roof and down in the street before the alarm was raised.

We went berserk that night. We all went mad, fuelled by resentment and the effects of the glue. We were crazy, and I did things I had never done before. I had the false courage of being in a group, and nothing mattered except the excitement. I robbed a young fella on the street, grabbed his stereo and scared him half to death. Then I snatched a woman's handbag; it was easy, I just grabbed it as we ran past, and she didn't even try to stop me. She looked terrified but I didn't care. When I discovered £90 in it I shared it with one other lad, a fella from my town, and told him not to let on to the rest how much we'd found. Those two crimes still stick in my mind; previously I'd never done anything which involved meeting someone face-to-face. Stealing, bomb hoaxes, criminal damage... somehow it seemed completely different from grabbing something from a person in the street. I hate to think about it even now.

We continued on the rampage, trashing our way across the town and out into the countryside; at Bangor we discovered a railway track and climbed down into the dark recesses each side and followed it. Railway tracks make a good alternative to roads when you're on foot because they're not lit and you become pretty much invisible.

At a place called Ballywalter we broke into a big house. I'd acquired a baseball bat along the way and we went to the front door and kicked it in, and I was waving the baseball bat around and shouting as we ran into the hall, only to find the owner of the house in front of us with a shotgun and the look of murder on his face! We turned and ran like crazy through the town until we came to a garage where we broke into the office and tipped out a tray of keys and tried them in the locks of the cars on the forecourt until one fitted. The six of us piled in, some of us still sniffing glue. None of us knew how to drive but we took turns, driving like maniacs, mounting pavements and taking corners too tight. How we didn't kill someone I'll never know.

Next we headed for Antrim because one of the fellas said he had a sister there whose house we could stay in. By now it was the early hours of the morning and it was much too soon to turn up on her doorstep, so we found a housing estate and took turns screeching around in the car, doing handbrake turns and bouncing off posts. The others got out and I was left, driving like a madman; in the end I wrecked the car by crashing into a tree. People woke up and peered from behind curtains. I kept thinking my time would run out and the police would appear, but amazingly they were nowhere to be seen.

Towards dawn a milkman turned into the estate in a wee lorry. As he delivered milk to each doorstep I jumped into his vehicle, intending to take it for a spin around the estate. I put my foot down on the accelerator but he'd left it in reverse and I shot straight back through a picket fence, into someone's front garden, mowing down flowers and coming to a stop in a clump of big shrubs. The milkman ran towards me, yelling and waving his arms, but the others had grabbed eggs from his van and were pelting him with them.

At eight o'clock we arrived at the sister's house, with a carrier bag full of alcohol. She wasn't as pleased to see us as we'd hoped. We stayed an hour or so until one of us threw up all over her sitting room. Then she chucked us out.

One of the group came from Ballyclare so we decided we'd go there next, and found a taxi. We jumped in, stinking of alcohol - me in the front and the others in the back - and asked for a particular housing estate. The plan was that when we arrived at our destination we would jump out and do a runner, but the others were whispering in the back of the taxi and when we stopped they ran off and left me to pay the fare. I said to the taxi driver: 'Hang on a minute, I'll just stand up and get the money out of my pocket'. 'Oh no, you won't', he replied, and reached over to grab me as I leapt out and ran off with him cursing me loudly. I ran down an alleyway straight into a clothes line that catapulted me onto the ground and I lay there dazed for a couple of minutes.

In the back of a bus station we finally ran out of steam. It was twenty-four hours since we'd run away, the booze and the money had run out and we were freezing. Rathgael suddenly seemed inviting. We decided to give ourselves up and traipsed down to the police station.

We'd left a trail of devastation behind us, from Bangor right through to Ballyclare. That night we committed between sixty and eighty crimes, but I didn't feel bad about it: the thought of what I'd done to those two people I'd robbed came much, much later. For now I was still on a high from the events of the night.

CHAPTER EIGHT

WILL IT NEVER END?

And so another year began without any progress in my life, or any likelihood of improvement, although after the rampage a lot of my anger had gone out of me and I was managing to keep out of trouble much of the time.

I spent my seventeenth birthday in Bangor Court where I was charged with absconding from Rathgael. Each one of us in the group who had trashed our way through the countryside appeared in court that day and we were all given twelve months in the young offenders centre. It seemed severe but it had definite benefits. It superseded the previous sentence, the one with the flexible charge ranging from one to three years. Now, with a sentence of twelve months ahead of me I could be out in six if I behaved myself. And at least this time I'd be in the young offenders centre with friends. Things seemed to be looking up.

We were still awaiting trial for the other charges hanging over us from that awful night, so every Wednesday we had to attend Antrim Court. Antrim was about thirty miles away so we were taken, handcuffed, from the young offenders centre in a prison van with windows. People in the streets stared at us as we passed. We stared back. It felt great.

I settled into the old routine and with time to reflect I began once again to try to work out what had happened. How come I was back in here when I'd resolved to stay out of trouble? Mmm.... now I thought about it, even six months was going to be a long stretch, and that was assuming I could stay out of trouble. Whatever else I did I must stay off the boards, because solitary counted badly against me and would affect my chances of getting out early. I must behave; I had no idea how to, except that by trying to keep my mouth shut I wouldn't be drawn into arguments and then into fights. I really felt my resolve strengthen. To know that I could be out in six months was just the motivation I needed, so I decided that nothing, absolutely nothing, was going to get me back in solitary confinement.

One morning at breakfast a Catholic guy from Belfast was serving the food, and all he gave me was bacon fat. I called him a name and he challenged me to a fight in my cell. I couldn't resist; it didn't even occur to me to resist. He beat me hard, punching me all around the cell, and it's funny the details you remember, but I had a big spot on my face, just the one, and he backed me against the sink, where the back pocket of my prison trousers caught on the tap. I couldn't budge. He came straight at me and punched me right on my spot and it burst.

Considering all the other fights I'd been in I don't know why someone bursting a spot on my face made me so angry, but I saw red and launched at him, ripping my trousers on the tap. I had him on the ground, with my fist raised above him, when the prison officers stormed in, and in less than no time I found myself heading for solitary again.

I got three days on the boards, lost two weeks remission and was prevented from going to association - that's the time in the evening when we could meet up to play pool and watch telly - for four weeks. They were much more lenient with the Catholic guy and that really annoyed me because if they'd walked in on us two minutes earlier they'd have found him on top of me, so he deserved the same punishment. But that's Murphy's law for you....

When it was time for the remaining charges to be heard against the six of us we were taken to the Crown Court. We went into a cell immediately above the courtroom to read through the papers from the Department of Prosecution, which listed the charges. Included in these papers were all the statements the police had assembled in evidence.

I couldn't believe what I was reading; one of the others in our group had told the police on all of us. And one name in particular stood out from the rest, appearing time after time throughout the document; *McCormick did this, McCormick did that; McCormick was here, McCormick was there.* It was all true of course, and I was fully prepared for whatever would be thrown at me for the things I'd done that night, but I certainly didn't take kindly to a friend telling on me. I leant across and smacked him in the face, hard. He made a wild noise and blood streamed out of his nose. The others piled in on him, and the six of us ended up in a tangle like a Chinese puzzle.

The racket filtered downstairs to the court and soon the judge was saying: 'Find out what's going on up there, will you?' and he sent the screws in to sort us out. It was just my luck that as they opened the door I happened to be the one with my fist in someone's face. Only one minute before that, all the others had been joining in... That moment of wild pleasure bought me another stretch in solitary and an extra month and a half added to my sentence.

In the end, the judge was very lenient, considering the number of charges against us. I left the young offenders centre with an eighteen-month suspended sentence hanging over me for two years; it could have been much, much worse.

I walked out of the prison gates without a backward glance. Again I felt like the local hero - to some of the younger boys in the town I probably was - and went straight to Ferris' Park where I knew my mates would be gathered. Some of the younger ones were still at school; most of them hadn't been in trouble, and they all crowded around to hear what it had been like inside. You can spin out the truth, make it sound really exciting. They were all impressed by my tales.

But that moment of glory passed and I had to work out what to do next. I was too old to go back to school and had no idea how to go about getting a job. I wasn't at all convinced that I could stay out of trouble; why would I, with my track record? I was back living with my parents, in their new house. I really didn't want to make things any harder for them; it had been awful for them, having me in prison, especially for my mother who'd travelled so often to visit me. I used to see the strain on her face and was amazed that she had even bothered to come at times. I went to the local job centre and they suggested another youth training programme; it would be a good way to pass time and get some money in my back pocket for drink.

I quite fancied becoming a chef, and was offered a placement in the kitchens of the local hospital. I had the potential to do well; I enjoyed the work and was good at what I did, but I was my own worst enemy. I still had a problem getting out of bed in the mornings. Unless I was in an institution with someone banging on the door and yelling, 'McCormick, get up!' I just couldn't raise my head off the pillow.

The people in the kitchens made me welcome but I'd barely got to know the ropes when I got the sack because I arrived every day at three in the afternoon instead of nine in the morning. The woman in charge of the kitchens had taken a shine to me; she must have seen something in me that no-one else did, least of all me, and she told me I'd worked well for the short time I'd been there, but she couldn't put up with my time-keeping. She said she was sad to get rid of me.

I'd let her down. I felt bad for a moment as I left the hospital but I pushed the feeling aside. I wasn't going to let emotion get to me; if I started on that I didn't know where it would end.

≋   ≋   ≋

I needed to belong somewhere, to be part of a group again, and it was around this time that I decided to join the UDA. I still looked up to the paramilitaries and felt a thrill every time I saw a march go past. They offered me things I was missing; excitement and a sense of belonging, and would surely fulfil this feeling of rebellion I lived with the whole time.

I knew that belonging to the UDA meant I would have to fit in, to comply with their rules. And to know when to keep my mouth shut.

CHAPTER NINE

WATCHING MY BACK

I made a good start; turned up regularly for meetings and made new friends. I strutted around town feeling proud that I'd realised an ambition which I'd held on to all that time since I'd fantasised about the paramilitaries as a child. Now I felt like a paramilitary; I felt accepted.

I started running around with the blokes in the UDA even though my usual group of friends were unpleasant to me because of it. The UDA blokes I was running around with held discos and we took turns to do the door; we weren't really bouncers, we just stood there to keep an eye on things as people came in. I was always drunk when I came to do my turn on the door on a Saturday night. Sometimes lads would come down from another organisation and we were always at odds with each other; we were all the same age, between sixteen and eighteen. I'd take them into the toilets and beat them up. I remember getting them into a headlock and battering and punching them. One night in particular the lads I'd fallen out with got fed up with this and about eight of them jumped me on the dance floor and one of them kicked me in the mouth; it bled something terrible and I ended up with seventeen stitches inside it. They kicked my tooth out, and I spent that Christmas with a big swollen mouth.

After a while I decided I didn't want anybody telling me how to run my life, not even the UDA, so I got cocky and started being mouthy. When I saw my UDA friends I was slabbering to them all the time, telling the commanders I think they're this and I think they're that. So I wasn't doing myself any favours, getting drunk every weekend and then worrying all week about what I'd said in case it backfired on me. I put myself through hell for month upon month like that, and then one night I was in the Rangers club on my housing estate and a fella who was in the UDA came in and tried to sit at our table. I didn't want him to and he moved away. I followed him out into the hall and we had an argument, and I said to him, 'Come outside and we'll sort it out,' and with that he just rammed a pint glass in my face and it broke. The main part went into my throat and I ended up with sixteen stitches across my neck. It was pretty sore but I liked the way people stared at it when I walked through town.

From then on it just got worse and I was slabbering and shouting and mouthing at weekends and asking for trouble. Then one night some fellas from the UDA were breaking into a shop and I just went up behind one of them and hit him from behind and they chased me. By this time I was skipping meetings or turning up late. Like in the army, if you don't stick to the rules they discipline you and that's what they did to me. I got my due punishment: shortly after that they came to the house the night I was playing cards. I deserved everything I got and it was amazing I got away with only a beating.

≈ ≈ ≈

After the punishment beating my personality changed dramatically. I was even more haunted by fear, more terrified than ever to go to sleep at night, listening for a knock at the door, scared to open my mouth. None of my fears was unfounded; next time I knew they would kill me and I'd have deserved it. This was real danger, and I didn't like it. I was stuck between a rock and a hard place. I'd never feared the police but I feared the UDA and what they could do to me. And I feared myself; I was no longer convinced I could keep out of trouble; in fact, I was absolutely sure I couldn't. My mouth and my temper were uncontrollable, but I was particularly afraid of my mouth. I saw now that when I had too much alcohol inside me I just had to open my mouth and all the wrong words would come out. My drinking was out of control; it had been for a long time, but now I was getting black-outs after only a few pints. Afterwards I'd have no idea what I'd said or done; for all I knew, during one of these bouts I could say some-thing about the UDA which would bring them back to my door, with a gun. I couldn't control my drinking; I couldn't control my mouth. I was in despair.

In my anxiety I thought about God and wondered if he was real. At my granny's house one evening I read about a guy from Larne called Rob Swan who got a life sentence and he became a Christian in jail and he had put an article in the religious page of the Larne Times. I got on my knees and prayed - I desperately wanted God to come into my life - but then the next day I went out drinking with my best mate, and thought: *How can I ever change?* I felt bad about myself; one minute talking to God, the next forgetting about him. I decided I couldn't have become a Christian after all, and forgot about it.

≈   ≈   ≈

Everywhere I went I waited for the UDA to catch up with me, and then a very strange thing happened which saved me from myself. I was arrested for a petrol bomb hoax which I hadn't done; in fact, at the time I was miles away from the scene. The police interrogated me very intensively; I was confused, depressed and desperate, so in the interrogation room I hadn't the strength to stand up to the questioning and I admitted to the crime. I was sentenced to two and a half years in the young offenders centre.

To my friends and family I pretended that the sentence bothered me, but really deep inside I was relieved because it had saved my life. It would take me away from Larne and all my connections with the UDA. I could disappear for a while. With remission I would be out after fifteen months, so that gave me a good long time to hide away and deal with the effects of the punishment beating. I had real hope

67

that I could work out where I'd gone wrong, and that I could change my ways. A respite was just what was needed, and it had come in the nick of time, courtesy of Her Majesty's Government.

Predictably, during the first weeks in prison my mouth got me into fights; some I got caught for, some I didn't, and I spent time in solitary. But I didn't care. I was safe inside, away from the UDA, away from myself. After a while I started to settle down, got into the routine and that's when another very strange thing happened.

Every Sunday morning I attended a church service inside the prison. It was something to do, to relieve the monotony of the week. Usually I managed to stay quiet, but nothing about it impressed me; the words and singing went right over my head. Each week a different speaker came into the prison to take the service, and then one Sunday I found myself sitting up and listening with more than a fleeting interest. David Hamilton was talking and my ears pricked up when he said he'd been in prison. He hadn't always been a Christian, he said, but Christ had changed his life and he would do it for us too if we were willing. I listened intently, although I made sure that my face stayed expressionless. A very peculiar thing was happening inside me, which I couldn't have put into words at the time because I wasn't used to dealing with emotion. Looking back now I would describe it this way: my heart, which had been dead for years, sat up and took notice, as if it had been breathed on or massaged and given a new lease of life.

There was something about David Hamilton that I couldn't quite put my finger on. He was obviously tough and I would have guessed from his face that he was an ex-con, but he had this real gentleness about him; not a softness, but a real kindness and compassion. You could feel it coming out of him; something from him went straight into my heart. I didn't wait to talk to anyone after the service; I went back to my cell and did what he had told us we could do - I talked to God. I said to him, 'I really want to know you. I've done so many wrong things, I'm really sorry for what I've done and I'm fed up with the way I am. Please come into my life and help me.'

David Hamilton was a born-again Christian, but I didn't understand what that meant, I wasn't interested in labels or titles, and I hadn't the first idea about the grace of God or mercy, compassion, forgiveness... or anything like that. But without any knowledge or forethought something happened inside me, and over the next weeks I found it easier to behave, without really trying. I had more control over my actions and feelings without needing to think about it; I didn't have to worry about controlling my temper.

I found that I wanted to get involved in the education classes, to learn the guitar and study English and Maths. I took up football again. I was very surprised, as were the people around me: in fact I was more than surprised; I was astounded at what was happening; this didn't feel like me! I knew it had to be God who was making the difference; I knew it was a real answer to that prayer I'd said. My whole behaviour took a turn for the better and I actually worked my way through the system to a house called Ash, which was for privileged prisoners. Gary McCormick, a privileged prisoner! Not in a million years would I have thought I could end up in Ash, and I did!

I had reached twenty; this was the age at which I'd expected my life to end. But it felt as if it was only just beginning, that there was something to look forward to. And, best of all, there was peace inside me.

Just before they moved me to Ash I was let out on a three day parole. Being outside again was a test, but I managed to get through the period without causing any bother. I did the usual things I enjoyed; I went drinking and picked up a girl, but the alcohol didn't lead me into trouble and afterwards I settled back into my work in the prison as easy as pie. The change in me was so evident I was given security clearance: this meant I could go outside the prison boundaries with the running and cycling teams - a fantastic taste of freedom and responsibility. I was also given a job in the gardens on the outside perimeter of the prison.

My senses began to come alive. I had a radio in my cell and one day I lay on my bunk listening to Radio 1: it was a lovely sunny day, the window was open a bit and the smell of newly cut grass wafted into my cell. It was springtime and I was due for a seven day parole. I was relaxed for the first time since... well, I couldn't remember when. In fact, I'd never felt so relaxed. I lay on my bunk and thought about my life. I was in the running, cycling and football teams, canoeing, doing the Duke of Edinburgh Award, I'd been given my security clearance... this was progress!

The end of my sentence was coming up, and I knew I'd need support if I was to continue being a Christian outside prison. I wrote to a ex-con I'd known in Larne, who'd become a Christian. I'd never been interested in him before, but now he seemed the right person to contact. He and a couple of his friends visited me and brought me a Bible; I tried to read it, but I found the Old Testament heavy going. I was quite interested in some of the main characters, such as Abraham and Moses, because they didn't always get things right, and you could see their lives were a struggle. I could relate to that, but a lot of it I didn't understand and I couldn't read it every day. Some of the fellas inside used Bible pages for their roll-ups but I had a bit more respect than that.

On my seven day parole I went to a disco feeling really happy; for me a completely new sensation. I didn't know you could have fun and not get into trouble! I met a girl called Jenny, a caring, kind girl with a warm smile. We saw each other every day till I went back inside. We wrote to each other and she visited me and I was really looking forward to getting out. My life was finally going somewhere.

The day I walked free at the end of my sentence Jenny met me and we went to the pigeon club and had a really great evening; drinking and eating and laughing. She was wearing a new outfit and looking lovely. I couldn't believe my luck in finding a girlfriend like her: she came from a very good family, she was sensible, had a full-time job and a car, and her parents were really kind. Jenny balanced me out; when I was with her I felt as if I had no cares in the world. I was actually happy.

I didn't bother to keep in contact with the Christians who'd visited me in prison. I was enjoying my new way of life so much I thought I wouldn't need them after all. It was the wrong decision; I depended too much on Jenny and after a while I started to get jealous. And then my thoughts started to taunt me: *Why on earth is she staying with you? You're no good for her*. I picked arguments with her. I'd not been in many relationships, certainly none as serious as this or with a girl as nice as this, and I couldn't handle how I felt about her. I wanted her all to myself, and every time she glanced at another man I felt insanely jealous. All my insecurities kicked in and we started to quarrel and drift apart.

I was trying desperately to be accepted and lead what I thought was a normal life but I was expecting too much, too soon. Without constant support, or the secure routine of an institution, I was still my own worst enemy. It was also difficult living back in Larne, because I had a reputation as a trouble-maker; a lot of people couldn't believe I had changed. As one of my mates said, 'A leopard doesn't change its spots, Gary.' To avoid seeing my friends I spent every spare moment with Jenny, and that put a lot of pressure on her.

I was fed up with living in Ireland; I needed a change. Jenny and I spent a week's holiday on the Isle of Man and liked it so much we made plans to move there, in the hope that our relationship would improve. I would spend a couple of weeks over there looking for work; once I'd found work she would join me. We told her parents, who thought it was a great idea; they knew how much I wanted to make good and were always really supportive of me.

I borrowed £500 from her father and around £200 from friends and family, got on the boat at Belfast as Jenny stood on the quay, waved goodbye to her and went down to the bar for a pint. And there I found a row of slot machines, the really tempting ones which pay out £100 at a time. I came off the boat four hours later with £30 in my pocket. When I realised what I'd done I panicked. I found a bed and breakfast place and asked how much they would charge for a week and was told £50; I offered £30, which was a laugh really, but this bloke was kind and he said, 'If that's all you've got I can let you have room only, but no food', I didn't eat for three days and I was determined not to go scrounging or stealing.

After the three days I was desperate for a drink and something to eat. I had 10p in my pocket. I went down to Douglas, to the slot machines on the promenade, and said a prayer. I said to God, 'If you're real you'll help me win', but the machine gobbled up my last 10p. I rang

Jenny and told her I'd been robbed but she knew me better than that, she knew I was lying, and wouldn't send me any money. I rang my parents and spun them a yarn. They probably didn't believe me either, but they sent me money to get back to the mainland.

CHAPTER TEN

'NEVER COME BACK HERE AGAIN!'

I was so desperate not to lose Jenny; she was my security, I was safe with her. I couldn't imagine surviving without her, but I'd blotted my copybook by lying to her so I was going to have to work really hard to keep the relationship going. I had another idea. I thought: *Maybe if we were both Christians...*

She agreed to give it a go and we went to church together for a wee while, but it just didn't work out. She wasn't really interested, and anyway we were doing it for the wrong reasons. Gradually I got bored with her and did hurtful things. One night I two-timed her and didn't care about how upset she was. We finally fell out in January, after eighteen months together.

I decided I had to get away from Northern Ireland. I had a mate living and working in London; I phoned to see if I could join him and he sounded really enthusiastic. He said, 'Aye Gary, come on over. I'll find you somewhere to stay.' I borrowed the fare for the flight from my parents, and took a job as a porter in a hotel near Larne for three weeks, for spending money.

I'll never forget how it felt the day I left Northern Ireland to go to London. The weight that came off my back was amazing. I could stop worrying that if I stepped out of line the UDA would be after me. Throughout the time I'd been with Jenny I'd cut down on the alcohol and had managed to stay out of trouble, but now I was on my own again and was still worried about the way alcohol loosened my tongue. It would take only one slip... But things would be different in London; I'd be away from my friends and familiar surroundings and my history. It would be good walking around without it mattering what religion you were, with nobody asking, 'Are you Catholic?' or 'Are you Protestant?' I could be a new person.

My first experience of London was memorable. My mate met me at the airport and we went straight to a pub in Earls Court. An hour later I was sitting at the bar quietly drinking a pint when this fella came up and accused me of hitting a girl in a Chinese takeaway in Walthamstow. Apparently it had happened three weeks previously. I tried to explain that I'd only just come over from Ireland, so it couldn't possibly have been me. He wouldn't listen and was about to give me a good hiding when one of the guys behind the bar recognised me and stood up for me; it turned out he was from Larne. He got me off the hook, which was a miracle because the last thing I needed was to walk straight into trouble. But when we got back to my mate's flat some guys were waiting for him with a grievance: they went for him, he moved out of the way and I took the punch. I ended up with a broken nose. What a welcome!

Some Irish friends at the Elephant & Castle fixed me up in their flat, and found me work as a labourer in Canary Wharf. I was twenty-two and suddenly I was earning £300 a week, more money than I'd had in my life. Much more than was good for me.

The work was hard; the hours very long. The day began at 7 a.m. and sometimes we worked through to midnight. You can't work that long without getting exhausted so I did what the others did; I took amphetamines to keep going. It was the first time I'd taken speed, and my boss thought I was a fantastic worker, seeing the pace I kept up for all those hours. My mates in the flat weren't so impressed; I couldn't sleep and was up all night taking baths and making a racket.

After a couple of months the work ended and I went back to Larne for a holiday. I was proud of myself; I was holding down a job, I'd enough money to buy decent clothes and I felt I was starting to gain respect from people rather than being known as a troublemaker. I met a new girlfriend and we got on like a house on fire right away. Life was good.

I'd planned to stay for two weeks but I let the holiday run on into a month so that I could spend time with my new girlfriend. Then I got a phone call from my mate in London who said he'd found some more work; 'There's good money to be earned, Gary, you should come back.' I hatched a plan. It was only seven weeks to Christmas, so if I went back to London, worked hard and saved £200 each week, I would have £1400 by Christmas. That would impress my girlfriend. The relationship had galloped along in the space of a month and we'd already talked about setting up home together; the money would make all the difference.

I set off for England again, and this time I could afford to pay my own way. As I crossed the Irish Sea and travelled down to London I had plenty of time to think and plan. Now that I was capable of holding down a job and earning some proper money I really believed I could make a new start for myself and this girlfriend.

I went back to work at Canary Wharf as a labourer; I got on well with the foreman and the other men on the building site, and spent a lot of time with them in the pub. We had fun, and I felt free. Somehow the idea of setting up home with this latest girlfriend didn't have the same appeal once I was back in London. I sent £200 home for the first week but then nothing.

Just before Christmas a letter arrived from the police, telling me that my grandmother had died and that my family wanted me to come home for her funeral. I was very upset; this was the granny I'd been really close to. I drank all day, smoked dope, and somehow or other got on the plane to Belfast and found my way from the airport to Larne where I went straight to the pub.

I woke up the next morning in my parents' house, and sensed a very strange atmosphere; I knew straight away that it was something to do with me. I found out when I went downstairs; apparently I'd arrived late at night when everyone was asleep, and in trying to find a way in I'd smashed all the windows at the back of the house. I'd been aggressive and completely out of control. My family had been so terrified that my twenty-year-old sister ran into my parents' room and slept with them. I was devastated at what I'd done. My grandmother's funeral passed in a blur; I couldn't feel a thing as they lowered her into the ground. All I could think was: *What on earth have I done, smashing my parents' windows?*

Later that day, my girlfriend came over to our house to talk about our future, and I couldn't raise any enthusiasm. I just ignored her. She was very hurt but I couldn't concentrate on her; I wasn't interested. I was heading back to England as soon as I could. The next evening I left for the airport in a taxi. My father stood and watched me go, and I had never seen his face look so grim. 'Don't ever come back to this house again. Do you hear me? Never come back.' In the taxi I stared out of the window as the familiar scenery passed by, but I saw none of it. All I could see was the pain etched in my dad's face as he'd said those awful words.

≈ ≈ ≈

After my dad rejected me my life went into a rapid decline. Until I could find somewhere to live I slept on the floor of my mate's flat: it was a dive, the place was rotten and stinking, like me. I managed to hold down my job, but every night I was drinking until I blacked out; I'd also started wetting myself when I was drunk. Most days I couldn't tell you what had happened the night before. One evening I picked a girl up in a pub; we were drunk when I took her back to the flat. The next morning I rolled over and saw that her face was covered in scabs and realised I'd picked up a drug addict. I told her to get out and she did, but only after she'd taken some money I'd left in the bedroom.

76

The foreman at Canary Wharf took pity on me and one day he said, 'I've been chatting to my wife, and we wonder if you'd like to come and live with us for a while, until you can sort yourself out.' It was very good of them, considering they had children, but I don't think they realised what they were taking on. They let me sleep on their sofa. I was still drinking every evening, and I started to wet the sofa and tried to conceal it from them. The wife noticed in the end; she didn't tell her husband but when the sofa starting smelling he told me that if I came back drunk again I would have to leave. The next night I came home drunk and they threw me out.

This time a mate found me some digs in the Wandsworth Road and the first night I came back drunk and threw myself down on the sofa and fell asleep; the next morning I couldn't believe that I'd wet it. There was no way to clean it up, so I poured beer over it and hoped the landlady wouldn't guess what had happened. The next night I slept in the bed and wet that, too. There was nothing I could do to conceal it and I knew that as soon as my landlady discovered it I'd be out on my ear.

I had spiralled out of control. I went into work the next day and my boss gave me a really hard time; I'd been smoking a joint during the night and turned up hung over and half asleep. I told him that I needed to go home and sleep it off. He said, 'You can't,' and I said, 'Well if you won't let me go home, I'll make sure we all go home instead,' and went into his office. I rang the police and told them that there were bombs planted in a tower block in Canary Wharf; one on the first floor and one on the sixth floor.

Before you could blink, the place was surrounded by police and I was arrested. It was six in the morning and it didn't take them long to find out who'd made the call, as I'd been the only one in the office with an Irish accent. I was in no fit state to say anything sensible so they put me in a cell and let me sleep till five that afternoon. When they questioned me I owned up to it right away; I had no idea how seriously they took bomb hoaxes in London. If I'd known, I might have thought of something a little bit less politically sensitive to get the attention I was craving.

CHAPTER ELEVEN

PLAYING THE HENCHMAN

Well done, Gary, now look where you've got yourself. You're in a bloomin' mess.

I was giving myself a right old telling-off as I walked down the Wandsworth Road. *You're in London, supposed to be making a new life for yourself. You're on bail, waiting for a court case, with no money and no way of making any. What are you playing at?* I nagged away at myself.

Later that day I was standing in a video shop when two fellas came in and one of them walked right up to me, though I'd never seen him before, and said: 'Do you want to earn £20?' I couldn't believe my ears. 'I might,' I said, ever so casually.

They'd heard about me through a friend of a friend who said I was just the person they were looking for; you know how it goes. They took me back to their flat and from the start it felt like a weird set-up. One of the guys, a much older fella, said, 'Right Gary, it's very easy. You're going to get back some money we're owed.' They explained what they wanted me to do and told me I would need to find myself a dark suit, a shirt and tie. I was to be a henchman.

We acted out the scenario so they could make sure I'd say the right things. 'You're to pretend to be the head of a drug team, Gary,' they told me. I'd never thought of myself as an actor, but once we'd run through the role a few times I was really getting the idea, strutting around like someone out of a low budget movie. I asked them why they weren't using someone they already knew. 'Well, Gary, it's the fact that you're new to the area. The most important thing is that we use someone who won't be recognised.'

The next evening I dressed up and waited in the flat with one of these guys, and in walked the man who owed the money. He took one look at me and said: 'I think I know you.' It could only happen to me. There I was in a city of millions, knowing not even a handful of people and this guy recognised me. A few weeks earlier I'd taken to getting famously drunk on whisky trebles in a karaoke bar in the Lambeth Walk, where I'd decided I could sing like a sparrow, and had grabbed the mike and sung my little Irish heart out. Not once, not twice, but night after night. Even by karaoke standards my singing was terrible. Eventually the landlord told me that if I sang again he'd throw me out.

He looked closely at me. 'Yeah, I do know you. You used to sing down that place in the Lambeth Walk.' I told him he'd got the wrong guy but of course he didn't believe me, so I had to start shouting at him. It was awful: there I was waving my fist in his face and threatening him that if he didn't pay up his family would be in trouble. He peeled off £700 in notes and left, and then I felt good about myself for a few seconds; after all, I'd carried it off. One of the blokes said, 'Well done Gary,' and gave me twenty quid and a wee bit of dope. Then he took me into another room and showed me a satchel with £50,000 in it. I couldn't understand why he was showing it to me, but I had the feeling I was about to get into something out of my depths.

These guys started grooming me, taking me out to restaurants and clubs. I liked it. I was flavour of the month and it felt good to be eating in quality places and having some proper attention. They fixed me up with a mobile phone; a novelty then, they were so rare. That really gave me status. I walked around with this big brick of a thing in my hand as if I was some sort of celebrity. Well, until the night I rang my mother when I was off my head with drink and drugs in a nightclub, and dropped the phone down a toilet and that was the end of that.

At times I really enjoyed myself. When I was wearing the suit, acting the part, I felt like the bee's knees. I thought I was doing a great job, but in truth I was a hopeless henchman; acting, and most likely looking, like something out of a kid's comic.

Gradually my life deteriorated into a twilight world of seedy nightclubs, double-dealing and drug-taking. I was mixing with some very dubious characters and I started to worry because in a lucid moment I reminded myself that I was out of prison on bail, with an imminent court appearance. With my track record it was only a matter of time before something went disastrously wrong, and if I broke bail I would be in real trouble.

And so I did a rare and, for me, wise thing. I took a good look at the whole situation from the outside and cobbled together a sensible thought: I had to get away from the net I'd tangled myself in for the sake of £20. The thought of going back to Ireland suddenly seemed very sweet, UDA or no UDA. I left London in the early hours one morning with my collar up, my head down and just a holdall to my name. I let out a huge sigh as I landed back on Irish soil and stood for a few sentimental moments taking in the air.

I wasn't welcome at my parents, but there was always someone who would put me up. My best mate's mum said I could stay with them, so I spent a fortnight at their house, watching telly, eating and sleeping. My mind was in a state; I couldn't get it to slow down. It was as if my head was full of squawking birds flying around in circles, chattering at me, and I couldn't get a hold of them to shut them up. My thoughts nagged at me again: *How have you got yourself in this state, Gary McCormick? You're on the run with only a bag of clothes to your name, when six months ago you were living with your parents, you had a nice girlfriend, you were doing normal things. You've managed a 360 degree turn in London and your life's in another absolute mess.*

81

I knew I was heading back to jail, yet I'd been so desperate to stay out of it. Why did things keep going so wrong? I was devastated when I stopped and thought about the progress I'd gained and, as quickly, lost. Round and round and round went the chattering thoughts.

I had no money, I wasn't going to resort to crime to get any and there was no work I could do in the short time I was in Larne, so when it was time to go back to London for the court case I begged the fare from a mate. The night I left Larne I was walking down to the dock to get the boat and passed a football pitch where there was a five-a-side competition. One of my mates was playing, and I stood and watched him for a few minutes. It all looked so ordinary, and it was comforting in a strange way. Someone scored a goal and there was cheering. Shortly they'd be off to the pub for a few pints and a laugh. I longed to join them.

But where was I heading? On another trek back to England where I hardly knew a soul; another journey back to court. I hadn't a decent item of clothing to my name; I looked a mess, I was a mess. Football, friends, the pub? I might as well aim for Planet Zork.

≈ ≈ ≈

I stood in court accused of a bomb hoax, what the law calls 'giving false information.' I was expecting to get three months, and when I heard the judge sentence me to two years I couldn't believe it and I had to hold on to the rail in front of me in the dock to steady myself. My spirits plummeted; English prisons had a bad reputation. My former boss from Canary Wharf stood in the gallery and watched me being taken away. I was touched that he'd bothered to turn up, after all I'd put him through.

They take you straight down to the cells from the court. No time for talking to anyone or going home for possessions. The door slammed with a thud and I was alone. What could I do but pray, and weep. I said to God, 'I know I got myself here, but please can you help me? Oh yes, I realise I've ignored you totally up until now, and behaved like a complete thug, but now I'm here can you do something about it? Please?'

They moved me on to Brixton Prison in the meat wagon, a very accurate name because you feel just like cattle, jammed in and herded from van to prison. Brixton is a holding place where they assess you and decide which prison will be the most suitable. This was my first time in adult prison and it was the lack of attention of any sort that I noticed more than anything. I'd have given my right arm to be shouted or screamed at; anything rather than being ignored, and processed as if I was an animal.

Two things are essential for survival inside: something to trade with and someone to get alongside. I was terrified at being Irish in an English prison for doing a bomb hoax, but I wasn't going to show it. I acted cocky, got friendly with a black bloke and traded the only thing I owned - a pouch of tobacco - for some dope; enough to make three joints, enough to take the edge off things and dumb down the panic in my head.

They put me on D wing, on the third landing, in a cell with a guy from Africa; a drug runner who'd been daft enough to get himself caught at Heathrow with a load of drugs inside his body. He couldn't speak a word of English and he smelt like rotten meat. He'd already taken the bottom bunk but I didn't care because from the top bunk I could smoke dope out of the window, which I could open just a bit. Conversation was impossible, all he could say was, 'Mm, mm,' so I just lay on my bunk in a haze.

Every prison has a different smell, and this was the worst I'd known. Every morning at let-out, when we emptied our buckets, there was this disgusting smell of urine; you wouldn't believe how many different types there are, as if there was a different smell for each nationality. It was revolting.

That week my name appeared in the national papers and on the ITV news. *Irish labourer gets two years for bomb hoax*. There was no way I could prevent my parents from finding out now, and that made me feel dreadful.

They kept me at Brixton for five days. The evening before I was due to be moved on I got talking to another prisoner about where we would be sent, and he said to me, 'Whatever you do, mate, don't end up in Camp Hill on the Isle of Wight. It's a discipline nick; it's where they send all the prisoners they can't cope with in other prisons.'

The next day they took me to the reception area and said: 'McCormick, you're in Camp Hill on the Isle of Wight. Leaving now.'

CHAPTER TWELVE

CAN'T CUT THE JUGULAR

It was a scorching hot July day when they took me off to Camp Hill, handcuffed and sardined into a prison van; this was the sweat box, and it made the meat wagon seem like a holiday home. There were no windows and we were stuffed in individual cubicles, with very little air. From Brixton they drove us to Southampton and on to the ferry. It sounded like we were in the bowels of the boat alongside the lorries and trucks. There was incessant clanking and shouting and then silence, with just the vibration of the boat's engines. I was petrified. What in Heaven's name was I heading into? How long would I last in an English prison?

I was numb as they processed me through the reception centre. Shower, prison uniform, identification number... I knew this routine well. It was done mechanically; I felt like a lump of meat in an abattoir. They admitted me to the induction wing for a couple of weeks, so that I could be assessed. I was on my guard, aware that they were watching me all the time, evaluating me, so I played quiet and withdrew into myself. This was no act; I was genuinely shocked that I'd landed back in prison. I was in a foreign land, both physically and inside my head. I didn't want to mix with anyone so I went into hiding, somewhere deep inside myself.

I was puzzled. I thought again and again about how my life had changed, and how I had regressed to the point of being back in prison. I deserved it; I wasn't debating the fact that I should be there, but however hard I tried I couldn't work out how I had let it happen. I couldn't get a handle on what was driving me to self-destruction.

Camp Hill was a grim prison, a terrible place; dirty, run-down, with a dreary atmosphere. It was like a Victorian workhouse, minus the luxuries! I hadn't a clue what I was facing: I'd heard a lot of stories about the stabbings and thieving in this place, and I wasn't sure I had the resources to deal with that sort of aggression. They allocated me to a section called James, where they put me in a cell with three other men. My life was reduced to one room, with two sets of bunks, a couple of tables and a wee sink and toilet.

We were given the worst prison food I'd ever come across; it was just masses of tasteless stew and puddings as hard as rocks. There's never enough to eat in any prison; it's not meant to be a holiday, is it? It's not as if you can go out and buy a chocolate bar or a snack, so you just last from meal to meal. Breakfast at Camp Hill would be one egg and a slice of bread and that would have to see me through till lunch. I was hungry all the time.

At night we were locked in our cells; for half an hour or so after lockup you heard people shouting from landing to landing, but soon everyone settled down and it wasn't difficult to get to sleep. The worst sound was that of the cell doors closing - a distinct heavy hard clunk; hearing that over and over again, up and down the landings, made me shiver. And there was the sound of the grilles between the landings being slid across. Such sinister noises.

There were fewer officers than I'd been used to, and that meant much less time for association, so I spent a lot of time in my cell. Although the prison was different from any I'd experienced before, I soon discovered that I knew the culture; I knew the language of prison better than any; who to steer clear of and who to get alongside; how to avoid trouble and when to become invisible. Drugs and tobacco were the currency and daily life revolved around trading them.

I gradually got used to this new situation; I began to fit in. I still kept my mouth shut as much as possible, though, and for the first time in my life I found it wasn't hard to do. After a while I realised that I was going to survive Camp Hill, and I started to come out of my shell.

Everyone was allocated jobs and I was sent to the sewing shop, where they put me on a sewing machine making boxer shorts, aprons and tea towels. It was piece work and we were given quotas to achieve, but I hadn't a clue about sewing; I was all fingers and thumbs, so my output was hopeless. A couple of black blokes in there were brilliant on the machines and they used to wheel and deal. They were old hands at it and in prison currency they must have been making an absolute fortune. 'Give us a half ounce of tobacco and we'll do your quota for the week,' they'd say. I don't know how they managed to keep it up, but it worked.

I could use the gym or play football on the artificial turf in the exercise yard but I couldn't be bothered. I was smoking pot every day and preferred to stay in my cell with my three cell-mates, getting stoned. No-one seemed to mind; the screws ignored us most of the time. Weeks became months and when Christmas arrived I stayed in my bunk all day, stoned. The screws came round with roast turkey, but I wasn't interested; I just lay there not caring whether it was Christmas or half past Tuesday. Someone had given me a quarter of marijuana, enough for about ten joints, and I smoked myself into oblivion.

Our cell came to life briefly on New Year's Eve; we celebrated by tearing the cupboards off the walls, breaking them up into small pieces and pushing them through the chink of a gap in the window, just wide enough to slide a hand through, sideways. The screws didn't seem bothered; they replaced the cupboards and life went back to normal.

For the first time I sank into a deep depression: it was less painful than looking at my future. I knew that if I rose above the haze of dope I'd see no end to the agony of my life. I'd be out of prison in so many months, but then what? What hope did I have of ever leading a normal life?

≈ ≈ ≈

17th March. I'll never forget that date, because it was the day when something happened which planted in me real hope for the first time ever. I'd kept my nose clean, and would be out of Camp Hill pretty soon, after only twelve months, but I wasn't looking forward to my release; in my mind my life had become unmanageable and I couldn't see how I would survive outside prison. I certainly had no expectation of being able to keep out of trouble.

Every prison had Bibles in the cells and on this particular day I'd picked one up absent-mindedly; occasionally when I wasn't smoking joints I thought about Jesus and how he made a difference to people's lives. Now that my release was approaching I began to panic; I was desperate to change the way I was, and in the cell I asked him to come into my heart. I knew I'd done this before but last time I'd ignored him once I left prison. This time I was more desperate than I'd ever been. I wanted to change because I really needed to change. I was lying on my bunk reading the book of Philippians in the New Testament and suddenly a verse came alive; it virtually jumped off the page and threw itself at me. It was very simple, all it said was, 'My God shall supply all of your needs in Christ Jesus' (Phil 4:19). I jumped off my bunk and bounced around the cell, and the other guys looked at me as if I was absolutely mad, but I didn't care. I knew, this time I really knew, that God was speaking to me personally and that he cared.

I came across other scriptures I knew were meant for me; '...that he who began a good work in you will carry it on to completion...' (Phil 1:6), and also Psalm 139:14, 'I am fearfully and wonderfully made.' I suddenly felt optimistic about my future in God's hands. I came alive. I stopped smoking dope and spent my time reading the Bible and talking to God in my head.

I had to start thinking about where I would go from here; on my release from prison I would be on parole and was required to spend some time in either a halfway house or a hostel. Most of my friends

88

were in Ireland and I didn't want to go back there; I couldn't imagine how I would fit into Northern Ireland as a Christian rather than with the Protestant label. I also wanted to avoid London. I didn't know, nor understand, enough about the Christian faith to stand alone in it. I had also neglected it badly; I desperately needed people alongside me, especially people who would tolerate me if I tried to reject them. But who was there? I had no friends in England I wanted to look up, and I knew if I went back to London I would get into trouble in no time. I would turn to drink again, and something inside me told me that next time I did that I would probably end up dead, not at the hands of the UDA, but by ending it myself.

I'd heard about a Christian halfway house in Preston. It was called Lydia House. I wondered why it was named after a woman and found Lydia in the Bible. In the New Testament it says that she was, 'a dealer in purple cloth from the city of Thyatira, who was a worshipper of God' (Acts 16:14). Apparently some followers of Jesus stayed with her when they came out of prison. I decided I would rather stay in a halfway house than a hostel; it sounded more like home. I applied for a place there.

People who become Christians in prison can have a really challenging time fitting into society when they leave, because they so desperately don't want to go back to their old ways. It's hard not to turn back to crime when you're outside again, especially if it's all you know. It's a very vulnerable time, and it's so tempting just to look up old friends and restart the vicious circle. The people who ran Lydia House were aware of the temptations and dangers.

I was interviewed in prison by a couple of people from the charity who run Lydia House. They asked me why I had applied to go there, and I told them that if I went to a hostel I was afraid I would turn back to my old way of life again; I was particularly worried about being tempted by alcohol. I soon heard that I'd been accepted, and I was so relieved.

The day I left Camp Hill was such a non-event: no youngsters crowding me to find out what it was like inside; no mates to meet down at the pub. As I walked through the prison gates and down the road to the bus stop I felt very deflated; I didn't want to be released. I would rather have stayed inside. Camp Hill hadn't turned out to be as terrible as I'd expected and now I was on the brink of moving forward again I didn't want to take the first step into the unknown.

It seemed a very long journey to Preston; first by ferry to Southampton, then by train via London to the North, and at no point did I feel excited. I nearly weakened at one stage and wondered about ringing a girl I knew in London, thinking maybe I would do a runner, but I didn't. As I was out on parole I would have to report to a probation officer in Preston; bending the rules required too much effort, so I got on the train and went where I was supposed to go. I felt like I had no choice but to do the right thing, as if something, or someone, was leading me.

The halfway house was just an ordinary home in a residential area of the town. There were four ex-cons, plus the houseparents, a married couple. They were kind people but they were new to this sort of work and maybe they were a bit too kind; I could see straight away that I would be able to wind them round my little finger. I needed a lot of structure to keep me either in line or motivated; self-motivation was something I still had to learn.

I wanted to fit in, I really did, and I tried to. I was twenty-three and truly wanted to get my life together, especially after my recent experience of getting to know God; I was in a hurry to put all my old ways behind me. I expected to see a big change in my attitudes and when nothing happened immediately I became bored and restless. I had been without a girlfriend for nearly two years and was desperate for a woman.

So I started going out in the evenings and again I began to slip, though this time it was very gradual and, in comparison with my life before Camp Hill, I wasn't that much harm to anyone. I became rebellious in small things: not keeping to mealtimes and getting in late at night because I was out with different women every evening. After a while I started getting drunk again. There was nothing in life that gave me a better feeling than alcohol and knowing there was a woman in my life.

I shouldn't have tried to rush this stage; it was supposed to be the beginning of a new way of life, but I didn't find it exciting enough. My depression continued and one night when a girlfriend finished with me I knew I couldn't face life any more. I decided to kill myself; it seemed the only way out. I had enough money in my pocket to buy five pints and I thought: *I know what I'll do. I'll just go down to the pub for one last time and then I'll come back here and cut my jugular vein.*

But God had other plans. I was standing at the bar drinking my fourth pint when a woman came over and introduced herself. She was quite good looking and I thought: *Why on earth is she talking to me?!* All I wanted was to be left alone, to finish my beer and go home and end it all. She said, 'Let me introduce you to my husband,' and then this man joined us and said, 'What do you want to drink?' 'Look mate,' I replied, 'don't think I'm being rude but I only have enough for five pints,' thinking: *Why don't these people go away?* And he said, 'Listen, don't worry about it, I'll take you out tonight.' So the next thing I knew, we were on the way to a Preston nightclub, and instead of killing myself I ended up paralytic outside a pastor's house, miles away, at eight o'clock the next morning, without any idea how I'd got there. He was the pastor I'd got to know since coming to the halfway house, and he had always tried to encourage and help me. I told him the story of the night before and the couple I had met. I never saw them again and have no idea who they were. But after that I didn't have the desire to kill myself. I may have neglected God, but I know for sure that he was with me that night.

CHAPTER THIRTEEN

IN AND OUT OF THE GROOVE

There was this barber in Streatham; I'd visited him a few times when I lived in London. While I was sitting waiting my turn I watched him walk from side to side behind the same chair, and I noticed that his walking had cut a groove in the vinyl flooring. He'd been doing this job for twenty years: day in, day out, he'd shuffled in a semi-circle, cutting, clipping, shaving. And those twenty years could be seen in the mark he'd made on the floor; his groove.

Watching the barber got me thinking about grooves. There's the groove made by water running over a rock face for years and years. Stone steps get grooves in them through constant use, and when a volcano erupts the lava comes down the mountain and hardens, leaving really deep grooves.

There was a really deep groove inside me, in my very inner being, which I couldn't remove. It felt like a kind of helplessness, and had

93

come from being institutionalised for much of my life. In prison everything was done for me; all I'd been responsible for was taking myself to the toilet! Once I was released I felt like a battery hen who'd been let out of its cage but who continued to walk around in a space a foot square because that was all it had ever been used to.

Although I wanted to improve my life I felt completely powerless; if I tried to make an effort by, say, setting myself a routine to pray or exercise or by deciding to stop drinking alcohol, I could only stick at it for a short time before I gave up. I couldn't handle responsibility, and whenever I failed I felt worthless and useless. I was stuck in a groove of low self-esteem, which seemed to be leading me to destruction.

I knew that only God could remove me from the groove, but I had to be willing; I knew he would never do anything without my consent. I asked God to get me out of my groove; sometimes I yelled at him, I was that desperate. I wanted a quick fix, and didn't see that he was answering me, that very, very gradually I was changing. I wanted an instant personality bypass, so that I could do all the things I really yearned to do; to fall in love with a woman, to marry and bring up children.

≈   ≈   ≈

The more I thought about it, the more convinced I was that God had sent the couple to rescue me the night I'd planned to commit suicide. It made me realise how much I meant to him, and also how much he must love me in spite of my personality. I began to think about him a lot more. I recalled the excitement I'd felt when that scripture had come alive in my prison cell, and started to read the Bible again.

'What a wretched man I am! Who will rescue me from this body of death? Thanks be to God - through Jesus Christ our Lord!' (Romans 7:24-25). I could relate to this passage. I was certainly a wretched guy, wanting to make good but unable to settle anywhere long enough to put down roots and build a stable life. But once again, just when I needed it, God stepped in to rescue me. Someone at the halfway house suggested I applied to Teen Challenge, a Christian rehabilitation centre for alcohol and drug addicts, based in Wales. The only way you could get into Teen Challenge was if you were in a mess, so that was no problem; I applied, and passed with flying colours!

Before I could start there I had to get funding. I went to the local council in Preston to see if they could help. They arranged for me to meet an advisor at a drug and alcohol advice centre that same afternoon, but I arrived with time to spare, so before the appointment I went down to the pub and had a few pints.

At the centre the advisor was very friendly and seemed keen to help, but he said, 'Gary, the only way to get funding is if you come in here with a needle hanging out of your arm.' I told him I wasn't a drug addict, so he thought for a minute, leaned forward and said, 'Ah, I can smell the drink. Why don't you go and see our alcohol counsellor?' So the next thing, I was talking to the lady who dealt with alcohol problems; when I told her my story she was very sympathetic and I got the funding.

Teen Challenge is based in Llanelli in South Wales, in a lovely rural setting. I enrolled on a course for twelve months, during which time I would live there. They explained that I would go through a series of studies, looking at many different aspects of addiction. I wasn't too excited at the thought of studying again, but I could cope with it because I knew God wanted me to be there. Don't ask me how I knew; I just had this feeling.

I learned so much at Teen Challenge. I liked it a lot; I felt safe there, knowing that the staff understood my internal struggles and my dependency on alcohol. I liked the structure, and because it was an institution I settled easily into the routine. I learnt things which would be wee steps for other people, but which were big strides for me, such as how to get out of bed first thing in the morning without someone shouting at me. Mind you, at Teen Challenge you couldn't doss in bed anyway, I tried it a few times but they wouldn't let me get away with it. I also learnt how to get to meals on time, and to keep promises.

The study time was very tough and I found it difficult to concentrate; I was constantly tempted away by weight-training in the gym. There were twelve different studies. We were asked to reflect on and answer questions such as: 'Who am I?' Now that was a good one for starters. Who the heck was I? I wasn't short of answers; I was a dead loss; an ex-con; a troublemaker, but now I could add that I was a child of God. I was supposed to see that as a positive thing, but it posed a real problem for me. The word 'child' bothered me; as a child I'd been very naughty, very sad or very fearful: thinking of myself as a child again didn't appeal to me. We also talked about God as our Father and I had to unlearn all sorts of concepts about what a father is. Because I had rebelled against my own father and been rejected by him it affected how I felt about God.

I had these mistaken ideas about God, which came from my grandmother, the one who'd given me a hard time about wetting the bed. She had called herself a Christian, but she had literally put the fear of God into me, and I couldn't think of God as being kind and loving. I had an image of a stern, grim-faced old-fashioned preacher, ready to tell me off at any opportunity. But during my time at Teen Challenge I learnt about his kindnesses; about his grace and mercy. I learnt about forgiveness, that it was best if I forgave people, both for their sake and for mine. A lot of people in our class struggled with that but funnily enough I didn't; I had been such an awful person and hurt so many people, the least I could do was to forgive others.

I could have run a mile when we started dealing with some of the emotional issues. During one study we looked at repressed memories, so that we could bring them up and deal with them by allowing the Holy Spirit to heal our emotions. I didn't even know I had repressed memories, and was surprised at what flooded back, most of them from when I was about ten years old, all of them painful.

The first was something which happened in Spain, where our family had gone for a holiday. One evening we went into Torremolinos for a meal. Afterwards we walked back along the road to our hotel in Benalmadena and on the way I started asking for a can of fizzy drink. At first no-one answered me so I began to nag and fuss. I was walking beside my dad and it was quite dark; I didn't see his hand coming so there wasn't time to duck. He hit me across the face and it nearly took the head off me; it hurt, really hurt. I'd had the odd cuff from him, and I'd deserved them, but he'd never hit me like that before; it was totally out of character. Emotionally I was stunned. I didn't cry; I just shut down and went into myself. I thought about it for years afterwards and the hurt cut into my soul, until it was buried deep.

Another awful memory was from the time when I was beginning to hang around with older boys. Before I got involved with those on Ferris' Park I used to trail around after a group from our estate who were about fifteen or sixteen. They made an awful mockery of me and abused me emotionally and physically. Just to earn the right to be with them I had to walk from one side of the road to the other a hundred times. They stubbed cigarettes out on my neck and once they kicked me in the mouth. Another time they stripped me in the cemetery and hung me by the ankles over the wall of the High School during sports day so everyone could see me naked, and all the kids on the school sports field watched and roared with laughter. I was hauled back into the cemetery and dumped on the ground. My face was burning with shame and I had to scrabble around for my clothes and pull them back on, while the boys mocked me.

I also recalled the day my father gave me £1. It was a lot of money for a ten-year-old; the first time I had ever been given so much. I was so excited I couldn't wait to tell my mates, these older boys that I hung around with. I remember it was a Saturday morning and I was going off into town to the Rangers club with my pound note. One of them snatched it off me, clipped me around the ear and sent me home. I was devastated but had no idea what to say or do about it.

We talked about these memories in class; we were encouraged to share how we felt about them, and given an opportunity to pray about the emotions they brought up - in my case, fear, shame and resentment - and ask God for healing. I felt better once I'd had the chance to pray, but I still felt shocked at what I had buried for so long.

I discovered that God could speak to me in different ways, that sometimes he would pass a message through someone else. Each morning a service was held in the chapel. Various people led the worship; one was a young Bible College student called Mark Davy. One day Mark said he had a scripture from God for someone, and it turned out to be me. I was so surprised! It said: 'May God himself, the God of peace, sanctify you through and through. May your whole spirit, soul and body be kept blameless at the coming of our Lord Jesus Christ. The one who calls you is faithful and he will do it' (1 Thess 5:23-24). In fact there was not one scripture, but two: '...being confident of this, that he who began a good work in you will carry it on to completion until the day of Christ Jesus' (Phil 1:6), which had also meant something to me in prison. I held on to these like treasures. I still do.

Outside study hours I managed to behave myself pretty well, except for one moment of rebellion when I drew two eyes on my backside, opened another guy's bedroom door and pulled my trousers down. One of the house rules was 'No horse play' so I was reported to the staff, but they turned a blind eye. I didn't think to wash the drawing off my backside that night. The next day we went to a public swimming pool and a group of school children giggled when they saw me in the showers.

I left Teen Challenge after nearly a year, but still didn't feel ready to live on my own, so when a couple who lived nearby asked me to stay with them it seemed a good solution. I soon discovered that their lifestyle was pretty unconventional. Their house was a shambles: the husband had a habit of starting DIY projects and not completing them; there was a big hole in the kitchen ceiling and their home was in a terrible mess. The wife did my washing but made sure that scanty items of her underwear appeared in among mine. I became increasingly uncomfortable about living there, then one afternoon I walked into the house when they weren't expecting me and found them sitting naked in the lounge, so I rang my pastor and he arranged to find me somewhere else to live.

The next place couldn't have been more of a contrast. I lived with a doctor and his family in a lovely rural setting, near a forest. They were very disciplined; I knew I had to fit in, and I wanted to because I liked and respected them. They were involved with walking puppies for the Guide Dogs for the Blind Association, so every morning I'd walk a crazy puppy through the woods. It used to make me smile to think what my old mates from Larne would say if they could see me! It was a pleasant and peaceful time, but it wasn't the real world, and eventually it was time to move on again. I wasn't looking forward to leaving. Unless there was someone constantly keeping an eye on me and organising my day I knew I would find it hard to sustain a normal life. I had help finding a bedsit, but I was very lonely after being with the doctor and his family for several months.

I started to feel very depressed; I had no job and no money, and was living on social security. I'd never learnt to drive and was regretting it because everyone I knew had a car and it gave them freedom. One morning I was in a mate's car, going round a roundabout, and suddenly I knew that God was saying that he wanted me to learn to drive! *Some chance of that, with no way of paying for driving lessons,* I thought, somewhat ungraciously. Later that day, out of the blue, I was offered a well-paid job working on the motorways, and I could afford to take driving lessons.

Fifteen months later I passed my test, on the seventh attempt, after seventy-two lessons. Talk about making a mountain out of a molehill! I'd learnt to drive quickly, but I was so nervous about taking the test that I went drinking the night before and each time I started the day with a hangover. By the time the examiner turned to me and said, 'Congratulations, Mr McCormick, you've passed,' it had cost me a bloomin' fortune, but I was delighted with the achievement. I had managed to maintain a job during that time and now I had a driving licence to show for it. This was progress!

CHAPTER FOURTEEN

SOMEBODY LOVES ME!

The years that followed were a real struggle: I came into the family of God, the church, swimming against the tide; I came as a rebel. Rather than listen to Christian friends, and there were quite a few I could call on if I chose to, I tried to do my own thing. It was hard to get my head around the fact that I didn't have to strive to be good. I was trying to reach the mark as a Christian; I still hadn't accepted that God's love is completely unconditional; that I could come to him with anything in my background or in my heart or mind and he would still want to know me. Once I started to realise what I had done to people and to myself my heart was full of pain, guilt and self-condemnation. I thought I should try harder and harder to behave and it just didn't work; in fact, the harder I tried, the more depressed I felt because I never seemed to reach my own mark. I kept moving my own goal-posts.

I had this naïve idea that the Christian life would be easy; that I'd be given good things on a plate. I'd have no more struggles, no more fears, get married, have a house, raise children. Life would be simple.

But it doesn't make that promise in the Bible. Jesus didn't lead a rosy life; far from it...

During my time at Teen Challenge I'd got to know Mark Davy well. Realising I was at a loose end Mark invited me to stay with him and his wife at their home in Cornwall. Mark had contacts with many young people through his church work and occasionally I had the opportunity to speak to groups of youngsters; they were very inspired by my story and loved to hear how different my life was from when I was in prison. But things weren't changing quickly enough for me and I felt guilty that some weeks I could be giving my testimony during a youth meeting, telling the youngsters what God had done for me, and then smoking a joint or drinking at the weekend. Alcohol was still my best friend.

I became restless and moved around, spending time in Manchester, London, Scotland... picking up work wherever I could, either with Christian organisations or using the painting and decorating skills I'd learnt in prison. I couldn't stay anywhere for long; sometimes a few months, sometimes as long as a couple of years. From time to time I gravitated back to Cornwall where I'd put down some roots, and did building work and odd jobs for people. But wherever I was I felt as if I didn't belong. I went to all sorts of churches as I travelled around the country like a refugee, looking for somewhere to settle; I mixed with all types of people, and still felt like the odd one out. That was how I saw myself; I wasn't prepared to believe that God could love me exactly the way I was, especially with the dependency on alcohol. Oddly enough, I'd understood how he'd loved me when I was a criminal, but now I was trying to stay on the straight and narrow I felt I was letting him down all the time.

But however despondent I felt at times God went on working inside me, and through me. I'd been a Christian for quite a while before I realised that my mouth was no longer getting me into trouble. It wasn't that I opened it less frequently - I'll have to be six feet under before I stop talking - but I didn't have the urge to argue any more and found that at times all I was compelled to talk about was God; It didn't seem to matter where I was, and some conversations began in the most unlikely places.

102

I like taking a sauna, especially when I've been to the gym. On one occasion in a Scottish leisure centre I became friendly with a group of blokes who used the sauna regularly. One of them asked me to go out on the booze with him, but I said, 'Look I don't drink much now, mate, because drink has made such a mess of my life.' I told him I'd been very dependent on alcohol and he asked how I'd managed to cut down on my drinking. I explained that I was a Christian and that I simply no longer had such a taste for alcohol, it just didn't give me a buzz as it had in the past, but because I still struggled with the temptation it was better if I avoided pubs.

He listened but didn't respond. He followed me from the sauna and in the changing room asked me lots of questions about God. I told him that I had a Bible in my car and he could have it if he wanted, and I was really surprised that he accepted it. I walked with him to his car and saw several books on the passenger seat, all of them about God and Jesus. I realised that I was just another link in the chain for him to reach closer to God.

On another occasion I went into a hotel sauna and found two fellas in the middle of a homosexual act - I was really angry and walked out, intending to report them because the place was full of children who could have walked in at any point.

They came into the changing room shortly after me; one of them put his clothes on quickly and left, but the other fella sat on a chair while I was getting changed and put his head in his hands and said, 'Look, I'm really sorry.' I was very tough on him because I saw that he was wearing a wedding ring, and I asked him if he was married and he said, 'Yes.' I wanted to feel angry with him but for some reason all I could feel was compassion, and I started sharing the gospel with him and gave him a Bible. I walked out thinking that if someone had offered me a million pounds at that point I would have rather shared the gospel with that bloke than had the money.

≈   ≈   ≈

For so many years the thing I've wanted more than anything is to be married, but I never seem able to keep a relationship going for long enough. I've had some lovely girlfriends but in the end I get jealous or bored.

One particular girl meant more to me than anyone else I'd met. She was called Anna. She was Swedish, ten years younger than me; I met her when I was visiting Sweden with a Christian group, and fell in love with her very quickly; she was beautiful with lovely eyes and that white blonde hair that the Scandinavians always seem to have.

She had been in a relationship for four years before we met and if I'd had any sense I would have put the brakes on, stood back and suggested she sorted out her feelings from the other relationship first, because I think that when we met she was still hurting from that. But I was head over heels in love with her.

I loved Sweden. The countryside was so clean and open and fresh, the cities exciting. On my first visit I arrived in Gothenburg and headed straight into the city centre; it was so thrilling, so different from anything I'd seen before, with the electric metro trains running through the streets. And the countryside... I couldn't believe the beauty. It stayed light late into the evening and one night I went down to a lake where there was a wee jetty, and I remember looking around and feeling the peace. Another very special memory I have was also by a lake, when the snow had fallen, and the lake was two feet thick in ice, and all you could hear was this crackling where the top layer of ice was moving. It was magical.

When I returned to England Anna wrote telling me she couldn't stop thinking about me, so I just dived in and allowed thoughts of her to consume me. I was so besotted with her, it felt like it was taking over my whole life and I was pleased about that because I was so desperate for a relationship. I went to Sweden for Christmas and stayed with Anna's family, and then she came over and visited me and suddenly we'd decided that she would move to England. It was a daft decision, made much too soon after we had met.

I've come to understand that God is not a killjoy; he really does want the best for us, but it took me a while to learn that lesson, and when he told me not to get into a physical relationship with Anna I ignored it. Before long we were in a deep, passionate relationship. We should have waited and got to know each other first.

And so Anna came over to England, to live in Cornwall where I was doing building work and odd jobs for people; she stayed with a family from my church. I'd really looked forward to her coming but the fun seemed to have gone out of our relationship. I was working full time, and not living close enough to her to see her during the day; she couldn't use her driving licence in this country so she wasn't getting out to meet people, and she became lonely.

I was having enough trouble coping with sorting myself out, without being able to empathise with her, although I really wanted to. Rather than seeing that she was unhappy and trying to help her through it, I thought that the relationship was turning sour and that she didn't like me as much as she had, and I became jealous and possessive. Anna was the sort of girl who would turn heads and I hated seeing other men look at her when we were out together. We started arguing every time we met, and couldn't sort it out between us, so she decided to go back home.

I was desperate not to lose her because at the beginning we had had such a fantastic relationship, so I suggested that I move to Sweden to be with her; hopefully that would improve things. I reasoned that maybe it was just because she was away from her home and family that things had gone wrong here. She agreed and I sold up the contents of my flat and moved to Sweden.

At first I lived with her parents and that went well, but their house wasn't big enough for all of us long term, so Anna and I moved into the family log cabin, which was nearby. As we were both Christians we shouldn't have lived together without being married; I knew it wasn't right, but I blanked out my convictions.

Our relationship had changed; we just couldn't recapture what we had at the beginning. In the mornings I went to college to learn Swedish, but my heart wasn't in it and I couldn't find the energy or enthusiasm to put enough effort into my studies. In the afternoons I worked in the community centre making wooden toys for the local kindergarten, but that wasn't satisfying me either. I was running ahead of God's plans for me, and nothing was working.

In the end a lot of the old Gary reappeared and my behaviour became atrocious; I was shouting at Anna and getting really angry, and I think it frightened her. My Christianity seemed to have flown out of the window again, but that wasn't surprising; I wasn't spending any time with God, I'd turned my back on him and put Anna first. Soon it was obvious I would have to leave, so I moved back to London and by then she didn't want anything more to do with me. I was very depressed; I felt like I had lost everything.

I took a job in a drug rehab called the Nehemiah project, as a full time Christian worker, but my heart wasn't in it. It was a stop gap after the end of the relationship, and eventually I just walked away from it, feeling I was letting down the people who'd employed me, but not able to care about it enough to stop myself.

Again I looked back at my life and tried to get a handle on what was going wrong; it seemed to me that since I'd been a Christian things hadn't exactly felt a whole lot better. I knew God was with me and I knew that he was using me, but I had expectations of what my life should be like, and I was angry that he wasn't giving me what I wanted more than anything in the world; a wife. I had no idea that there was more work to be done inside me.

CHAPTER FIFTEEN

REFLECTIONS

After my relationship with Anna failed I tried not to blame God for what had gone wrong; I could see that it was my fault. But sometimes I did feel that he wasn't listening to me because I had so badly wanted a wife and now I seemed further away than ever from finding one. Then I read somewhere that it's all about his timing and just because he doesn't seem to be answering prayer doesn't mean he isn't going to; it probably means that the time isn't right yet. He might be saying, 'No, Gary, not yet.' It made sense when I thought about it.

I had good days and bad days: on the bad days I felt that God had given me lots of opportunities and that I'd wasted, or missed, them; opportunities to get married or to get a new career. I looked back on an occasion when I was working in a drop in centre in Manchester with drug addicts; I could have made something out of that job, but I messed up because I could never stick at something for long, maybe because I haven't had consistency in my life.

I still drank from time to time, and one day when someone asked me,

107

'When do you feel happy, Gary?' for a minute I felt a real longing for alcohol again, to go out and get drunk, because that's when I used to feel really happy; a few pints inside me stopped me from feeling inhibited and scared. I'd also feel happy when I was on the move or preparing to travel; in effect running away, but I eventually realised that I was only running away from me, and that wherever I went, I met myself there! I was happiest whenever I was in a relationship with a girlfriend, as long as she was happy, that is! But after Anna I realised that I needed to get used to being happy on my own - I've never known how to do that. I prayed, and God began to show me how.

Other things that used to make me happy years ago - messing around with my mates, playing the fool - well, I'd grown out of those when I realised that I had to face the reality of life, the pain. Now, I had to learn how to build new friendships and long-term relationships, and begin to trust people. I had to make myself do that otherwise I knew I would tuck myself away. Like someone said, 'You make a prison for yourself Gary because that's what you're used to.'

Once I started thinking about relationships I realised that I even found ordinary friendships quite painful because sometimes I felt very weak as a person and didn't think I had anything to give; when I tried to make conversation with a new friend my mind went blank and I didn't know what to say. Odd, considering I wasn't usually short of words! But it was as if there was a blockage there, something which stopped me from getting too close to people, maybe a defence mechanism to stop me from getting hurt. It kicked in without me even knowing it.

I decided that a lot of it was about being accepted. Any man picking up this book would want to be accepted, wouldn't he? As a man it seems that you want to be with the in crowd; you want other men to think you've got it all together... that's what stops men being real with men. Even in church I wondered if men were being real; everyone seemed so successful and 'together'.

I'll never forget a guy I met in a halfway house; he'd come out of prison after a very long sentence. He felt that nobody accepted or understood him and eventually he threw himself in front of a train in

Preston station, yet a month before that he had said to me that he didn't have the guts to kill himself. He had thought people were talking about him, but I knew they weren't. After spending so long in jail you become institutionalised and that can make you paranoid, so you begin to think that people are talking about you. You hate yourself inside and you think that's what people see and so you think that people hate you, too.

It all seemed so complicated, and sometimes I'd say to God, 'Take me, I've had enough,' and then I'd think: *What if he does?* And then I'd panic! I couldn't win! I knew that God knew absolutely everything about me, that there was nothing I could hide from him. The word of God says, 'The Lord knows the thoughts of man' (Psalm 94:11), but I didn't always like that idea, and sometimes I felt like getting in the car and going away and starting all over again, somewhere where people wouldn't find me. But I knew it wasn't the answer, and realised that simply by staying in one place I was making progress.

At times I was really angry with God and sometimes I even cursed at him. I knew it wasn't right but I had to do it because I got so frustrated. One day I was reading a Christian book; it was really interesting and I knew that what it said was right, but it talked about men's emotions and I recognised myself; it made me so angry that I flung the book across the room. It was just what I needed to hear but I didn't want to listen. I fought against myself constantly, but I knew I had to move forwards, and at times I was making progress but couldn't measure it. Making progress felt like such a struggle, and I'd expected it to be easy.

I was determined to give myself a hard time, even when things improved. I began to control my drinking and should have been pleased about that, but instead I started to tell myself that I wasn't spending enough time in prayer or reading the Bible. Sometimes I just didn't bother to pray, and at other times chose not to, as if I was rebelling. Some days I wanted to be co-operative and other days I was deliberately stubborn. Often I felt as if there was a child inside me, still.

I was over-sensitive to everything and it was difficult to know where to start to sort it out. So I just stayed in Cornwall, kept my head down and got on with my work, and hoped and prayed that God would send something along to help me make a huge leap forward.

CHAPTER SIXTEEN

WHAT VOW OF SILENCE?

Me, ex-UDA and in a Roman Catholic monastery? A very unlikely combination.

When I heard that the BBC were looking for five men from all walks of life to be filmed living in a monastery for six weeks I applied, along with around six hundred others. I thought that taking some time away from my day-to-day life would give me a chance to find a vision, and time to meet God properly. I hoped it would make a difference to my future, maybe even set me on some sort of different path.

I was surprised to be told I was on the short-list. A series of interviews followed, and then I forgot about it. A few weeks later I was speech-less when I received a letter saying that I had been selected. God has a sense of humour, putting an Irish Protestant in a Catholic monastery.

The monastery was based in Sussex, in beautiful rolling countryside adjoining a public school. I didn't know what to expect; I imagined that the monks would be very different from ordinary people. I couldn't picture them smiling or having fun, or even talking to each other as people in the outside world did. So I was surprised to discover that not only were they affable and down-to-earth, they also mixed in the outside world; they had jobs in the community as nurses, youth workers or airport chaplains.

The four other men selected were different from me; all better educated, as were the monks. We were to live in the same community for six weeks, and because we would spend so much time together it was obviously important to build friendships. We had individual bedrooms, very nicely furnished, not the sort of cells I imagined monks had, and ate in the refectory with the brothers; the meals were superb because the chefs cooked for both the monastery and the public school.

Our day started at 5.30 a.m. and we went to church six times a day. Although there was no television or the sort of entertainment I was used to the days flew by and there was no time to be bored; when we were given spare time we were very appreciative of it. Sometimes I would lie on my bed and think about my life, or take a walk in the grounds.

Part of each day was set aside for study. We learnt about humility, obedience and silence, spending two weeks on each section. No points for guessing which I found the hardest! Not that I'm particularly good at humility or obedience, but I found it much easier learning about those than dealing with silence. The monks put a big emphasis on silence and I began to understand why. It's terrifying, because in the middle of silence you have to face yourself and you learn a lot about who you are. I discovered that I'm afraid to build relationships.

It takes years of discipline to be able to stay silent and have peace of mind at the same time. I found that even with my mouth shut I couldn't stop my mind from revolving, trying to sort things out all on its own. It wasn't difficult to keep quiet in the chapel, but we were also supposed to maintain silence between times of prayer when we took a break. We used to stand around outside the chapel and have a cigarette, and it was then that I just had to chat. The monks were so patient with me.

During the times when I managed to keep quiet I tried, as ever, to work out where my life had started to go wrong, but I still couldn't pinpoint where or how my problems had started. I looked right back through my life and saw myself like a ball in a pinball machine, jumping from side to side. I could feel real emotional pain - at times I just wanted to burst into tears - but I didn't know the reason for it. I still don't, but I trust God enough that I know he will show me one day, when I'm ready and able to deal with it.

When I was in the monastery I felt kind of free for the first time ever; I had so much energy. And God spoke to me. We were allocated mentors, and one day I went to see mine because I was beginning to feel that people were talking about me. I was actually making good progress but the paranoia threatened to return.

As I went to the final service of that day I was thinking about the things that were going round in my mind, and I thought, *I wonder why they never mention the devil, the evil one, in here?* With that, one of the brothers stood up and read this scripture: 'Be self-controlled and alert. Your enemy the devil prowls around like a roaring lion looking for someone to devour. Resist him, standing firm in the faith...' (1 Peter 5:8-9). No-one else had known what I was thinking, so I knew these words were from God and that he was on my side, however much I felt I was letting him down. It was a real endorsement and I felt very encouraged.

The structure and routine of the monastery day reminded me of prison, and I realised that I would fit back inside without any problem. But I knew that there was no chance of me going back to jail; God got in the way of that. *Still*, I reflected in the quiet times, *I would quite like to be back there. It would be tough but at least there'd be no responsibility; someone would organise my day, cook my meals...*

I nearly managed to get through the six weeks without incident, but one of the other men in our group got on my nerves after I'd lived with him for a while; he said things which seemed arrogant to me. In particular, he criticised the Bible without having ever read it, and that made me angry. How can you judge a book when you haven't even looked at what's inside it? My temper frayed and I had a stand-up argument with him. I wouldn't even have mentioned this momentary lapse had it not been filmed and broadcast to a few million people! You may well have seen it!

At the end of the six weeks one of the brothers said in his summing up speech: 'He should be called garrulous Gary because he never stops speaking.' I laughed; I didn't know what garrulous meant but it sounded funny, and I certainly knew he wasn't being unkind. Those monks had loved us and served us, just as Jesus would.

≈ ≈ ≈

I'd like to be able to say that after the monastery life was great, but it wasn't; I'd loved the excitement and the media attention, but once I was back in Cornwall, at work, leading a humdrum daily existence I slipped into depression again. I felt terrible and at first I thought nothing had changed. But this time I discovered that 'terrible' is sometimes OK, even necessary. I stopped taking antidepressants and let myself go through the pain that I still felt inside. I also tried to give up cigarettes; I'm hopeless at doing that, though as this book goes to print I haven't smoked for several weeks.

So things are looking up and I'm getting better at handling the negative moments. Sometimes I get bad dreams where people reject me, but once I'm awake I don't let them hammer my head; I try to ignore them. I'm learning to 'Give thanks in all circumstances' (1Thess 5:16-17). Since I've been doing that, life has changed for the better. Well, maybe life's no different, but my thinking is; the battle's in the mind, it's all in the mind.

I can look myself in the mirror now and say: *Gary, you're not doing too badly. You can get out of bed in the morning, get yourself to work and hold down a job. You've stopped drinking and taking drugs, haven't committed a crime in fifteen years and have stopped smoking, more or less.* Small achievements in comparison with some, when I look around and see the 'successful' people in the world, with families and careers. But huge steps for me.

I don't beat myself up as much as I used to. I'm no psychiatrist but I can see now that for most of my life I've been trying to fill gaps. I still have days when I think I'm pathetic and I focus on the fact that I've made so many mistakes and never seem to achieve anything. On those days I look around at the people I know and it seems that their lives are a lot further on than mine. And then when I'm feeling more positive I remind myself that everybody has struggles, and that I'm doing OK. I am often lonely, even though I have friends I can turn to. I know I'm not the only person in this situation but when you're on your own it's difficult to imagine how it is for anyone else. Sometimes I get angry with God because I haven't got married. But I get over it.

If I'm to believe the word of God, which I do, then I've been put on this earth for a purpose. I can't see what that purpose is at the minute, but I have a couple of ambitions; I'd like to work with young people again one day and I'd like to go back to Sweden. But for now I know I must stay put in Cornwall and work things through. There are still things in me which I would like God to change. For instance, there are times when I find social settings really difficult and I feel right out of my tree. I can stand up full of confidence and give a speech to a room full of people, but then be in a sitting room with just a small group and feel really inferior. It often happens in a family situation and maybe it's ghosts from the past; I don't know. But I would like it to change. And there's the fear... I said at the beginning of the book that I have always lived in fear. That fear is still in me today. One day I would like to walk around without it following me.

When the publisher started talking to me about this book I told him that I wanted to come across as real to the people who were reading it. Nothing I've said has been false, though I have left a lot of people out because I didn't want to identify them; I haven't exactly mixed with an elite crowd at times! I'm not ashamed that I've been to prison, because I've paid my debt to society, but I regret that I ever hurt people, especially my family.

It was strange doing this book, because I can't see that I've had anything special to say, except to be honest about how I feel. I'm not afraid to put across all my fears and my struggles and never mind owning up to what I've done. Even since I've been a Christian I've made a lot of mistakes with drink and women, but I keep going back to God for forgiveness and ask him to help me not to make the same mistakes again.

It helps me to read the Bible when I feel I've got things wrong because it's full of people who, like me, made mistakes and had a tough life. I like reading about Joseph in the Old Testament because he persevered, even when everyone was against him - his life was hard. I also like Elijah because he was so real; he did great feats for God and then curled underneath a tree and said, 'Lord get me out of here, I'm depressed.' I like David; God said he was a man after his own heart. All these men made mistakes, even Moses. If you read about them you find that none of them led a perfect life, in fact they were pretty hopeless at times. But God never gave up on them and with his help they achieved amazing things.

Someone asked me recently if I had a motto: I had to think about it, but I reckon it would be: *Just try. Persevere.* I try not to give up, I try to keep going for as long as I can. Sometimes I've felt like giving up and taking a load of tablets but I haven't; God has his hand on me and my life.

Since I was in the monastery something very good has happened. I have stopped drinking. For most of my life, since my first beer at the age of eleven, alcohol has been my lover and my enemy; it's given me some great fun times with my mates but it's also got me into loads of trouble. This year on my birthday, March 12th, I went away with friends and had a celebration without getting drunk, for the first time. And I enjoyed it!

These days I'm beginning to come out of my groove and look outside myself. When I manage to stop looking at my problems I see the most amazing things. I notice the patterns in wood, especially wood that's been made into something, like a turned bowl or a vase. And sometimes a nature programme on the telly will move me, such as when I see all those creatures that live at the bottom of the sea, to think that God took the trouble to make them so beautiful even though most of them are never seen by anybody. Then when I helped with the lambing on a farm I was mesmerised because when the baby sheep came out it knew exactly what to do; it went straight to its mother's teat, and

I thought: *How can that know what to do, when it's never been in the world before?*

The other day while I was reading my Bible I looked out of my window and there was a hawk hovering above the field opposite. I was really moved because I'd just been reading one of my favourite passages; it's a brilliant scripture...

'Do you not know? Have you not heard? The Lord is the everlasting God, the Creator of the ends of the earth. He will not grow tired or weary and his understanding no one can fathom. He gives strength to the weary and increases the power of the weak. Even youths grow tired and weary, and young men stumble and fall; but those who hope in the Lord will renew their strength. They will soar on wings like eagles; they will run and not grow weary, they will walk and not be faint' (Isaiah 40:28-31).

I feel like that eagle today because I'm beginning to see that now I can rise above my situations, whatever they are. I know now that situations often won't change, and if they do, things don't always get better. I know that I've still got things to fight through, and to battle on with my weaknesses. I know I still open my mouth and put my foot in it! But I'm different now. I've got a new perspective, and I know for certain that there's something better around the corner...

POSTSCRIPT

I regret all the crimes I've committed, all the bad things I've done, and all the pain I've put people through and I'd like to say sorry to all the people I've hurt.

I want to say a big thank you to the people I've worked with, and to all my friends for being there for me over the years. I don't need to name them because they know who they are. I really appreciate what they've done for me. I would also like to thank Sue, who wrote this book, for her patience, and Mike, the publisher, for his support and all his hard work.

But most of all I want to say thank you to my parents. Over the years I've caused them a lot of pain in all sorts of ways. I'm grateful that they are my parents and that they stuck by me through the years of pain, and I'd like to say thanks mum and dad for not giving up on me, and that I love you.

Gary McCormick

CONTACT PAGE

The publishers hope you have enjoyed this book.

Gary McCormick can be contacted as follows:

Gary McCormick
PO Box 109
Liskeard
PL14 4WW

Email: Garysbook@hotmail.co.uk